# VOTING BEHAVIOR

Other Books in the At Issue Series:

# VOTING BEHAVIOR

David Bender, *Publisher*
Bruno Leone, *Executive Editor*

Scott Barbour, *Managing Editor*
Brenda Stalcup, *Series Editor*

Paul A. Winters, *Book Editor*

An Opposing Viewpoints ® Series

Greenhaven Press, Inc.
San Diego, California

Library of Congress Cataloging-in-Publication Data

Voting behavior / Paul A. Winters, book editor.
     p.    cm. — (At issue)
    Includes bibliographical references and index.
    ISBN 1-56510-413-7 (lib. : alk. paper) — ISBN 1-56510-412-9
(pbk. : alk. paper)
    1. Voting—United States. 2. Elections—United States.
I. Winters, Paul A., 1965-  . II. Series: At issue (San Diego, Calif.).
JK1976.V67   1996
324.973′092—dc20                              96-13527
                                                   CIP

# Table of Contents

# Introduction

The percentage of eligible voters participating in presidential elections has declined markedly since the 1950s and 1960s, even though the total number of citizens casting votes has increased steadily over the years. This seeming discrepancy is explained by the fact that the number of Americans who are eligible to vote has expanded rapidly while the number who actually register and vote has not kept pace. In looking at the large numbers of people who do not vote, and at evidence that other forms of political participation have languished, many political scientists find reason for concern about the health of the American political system. They argue that Americans have become cynical about politics and distrustful of government, and a few contend that this distrust stems from the failure of political parties to attract and include the large numbers of new voters. These observers warn that such trends could lead to the breakdown of democracy. But other social scientists do not share this pessimism about the condition of American democracy, maintaining that simple reforms in the electoral process could encourage voters to participate in greater numbers. Further, Democrat and Republican partisans have a great deal of confidence in their respective parties' ability to draw support and votes and to restore Americans' faith in government.

## Lost faith in democracy?

A number of political scientists contend that the high level of nonvoting in the United States is a sign that Americans are losing faith in democracy. Harvard University professor of international affairs Robert D. Putnam agrees, noting that Americans' participation in all forms of political and civic organizations has fallen off dramatically since the 1950s. He finds that churches, labor unions, fraternal organizations (such as the Shriners, Jaycees, and Elks), volunteer organizations (such as the Red Cross), parent-teacher associations (PTAs), and other such organizations that encourage participation in community affairs have all experienced significant reductions in their memberships. For Putnam, this "is striking evidence . . . that the vibrancy of American civil society has notably declined." Putnam concludes that this erosion of what he calls "social capital"—social affiliations that support citizens' democratic attitudes—fuels rising distrust of government among Americans, which leads to their withdrawal from politics.

This rising distrust of government, which is consistently expressed in public opinion polls, is a source for concern, according to Seymour Martin Lipset, professor of public policy at George Mason University in

Fairfax, Virginia, but it does not signal that Americans' faith in democratic society is in danger. "Most Americans remain highly patriotic and religious [and] believe that they are living in the best society in the world," he asserts. Rather, Lipset contends, the erosion of voters' confidence in government is the result of the decline of political parties—their inability to incorporate the large numbers of new voters and to formulate policies addressing citizens' concerns. In his view, political parties are the primary tools with which citizens choose representatives and influence policies to address social problems. Because fewer voters are identifying themselves as either Democrats or Republicans, the political parties have weakened, undermining government's ability to respond quickly or effectively to problems identified by Americans, he argues. Lipset maintains that it is this "gridlock" that leads to the decrease of Americans' trust in their government, which in turn produces the spiraling decline in voting and other forms of political participation.

## Getting out the vote

Other political scientists dispute the idea that declining voter participation is a response to the state of American politics and the platforms of political parties. Ruy A. Teixeira, author of *The Disappearing American Voter*, contends that the increasing cynicism about politics and the distrust of government expressed in public opinion polls have little to do with declining turnout. Instead, he argues, voters are every bit as cynical and distrustful as nonvoters. "Someone who doesn't trust the government is no less likely to vote than someone who does trust the government," he asserts. Teixeira maintains that indifference to politics, rather than distrust of government, is the main reason Americans do not vote. He advocates political reforms that he believes would motivate more Americans to vote. Chief among the reforms that he supports is making voter registration easier. The decision not to vote is almost always the result of a decision not to register, he contends, so registering a greater number of citizens would encourage people to vote and raise levels of political participation.

In addition, Democratic and Republican partisans defend their respective parties' abilities to mobilize voters in support of policies and agendas. Republican activist Grover Norquist, president of the conservative Americans for Tax Reform, maintains that the results of the 1994 congressional election—in which a Republican majority gained control of both houses of Congress for the first time since 1944—demonstrate that voters enthusiastically support the Republican party and its legislative agenda. Norquist holds that government intrusion into the lives of citizens—mainly in the forms of taxation and regulation—is the cause of Americans' distrust in politics and government. He believes that the Republican program of lowering taxes and reducing the size and scope of the federal government will restore voters' trust in the political process. Speaking for his party, Democratic National Committee pollster Stanley B. Greenberg points out that the 1992 presidential election produced both a Democratic president and Democratic majorities in the House of Representatives and Senate. Greenberg believes that government actions and programs to protect working and middle-income citizens' standard of living will restore Americans' faith in government. With a platform that addresses middle-class economic concerns, he argues, the Democratic party can get voters to the polls in future elections.

Despite partisan enthusiasm, many eligible voters do not bother to cast their ballots. Whether this situation can be (or needs to be) remedied is a continuing topic of debate among politicians and political scientists. *At Issue: Voting Behavior* explores not only the reasons why some Americans do not vote, but also the factors that influence the decisions of those who do vote.

# 1

# Americans Are Losing Faith in Democracy

## Jean Bethke Elshtain

*Jean Bethke Elshtain is the Laura Spelman Rockefeller Professor of Social and Political Ethics at the University of Chicago and is the author of* Democracy on Trial.

American democracy is threatened by the declining participation and growing cynicism of voters. One reason for the decline of America's democratic civil society is the tendency of citizens to resolve political disputes in court. Court-imposed solutions to political problems produce a "politics of resentment" and preclude the deliberation and consideration of issues, by citizens and legislators alike, that maintenance of a democratic culture requires. Other reasons for the decline are the widespread use of opinion polls by legislators and proposals for "electronic democracy," a concept that would further erode democratic debate and political participation.

Liberal democracy is in trouble in America. Experts and ordinary citizens lament the growth of a culture of mistrust, cynicism, and scandal. Although a dwindling band of pundits and apologists insist that Americans are suffering the pangs of dislocation en route to salutary change, even progress, such reassurances ring increasingly hollow. The evidence indicates a growth of corrosive forms of isolation, boredom, and despair, declining levels of involvement in politics from simple acts such as the vote to more demanding participation in political parties and local, civic associations, an overall weakening, in other words, of democratic civil society.

Social scientists who have investigated the sharp decline in participation argue that the evidence points to nothing less than a crisis in "social capital formation," the forging of bonds of social and political trust and competence.[1] The pernicious effects of rising mistrust, privatization, and anomie are many. For example, there is empirical support for the popularly held view that where neighborhoods are intact, drug and alcohol abuse, crime, and truancy among the young diminish. Because neighborhoods are less and less likely to be intact, all forms of socially destructive

Jean Bethke Elshtain, "The Loss of Civil Society and the Decline of Liberal Democratic Faith," in *A New Moment in the Americas*, edited by Robert S. Leiken (Coral Gables, FL: University of Miami North-South Center; dist. by Transaction Publishers, 1994). Reprinted with permission.

10

behavior are on the rise. Americans at the end of the twentieth century suffer from the effects of a dramatic decline in the formation of social bonds, networks, and trust coupled with a diminution in investment in children. Children, in particular, have borne the brunt of negative social trends. All one need do is look at any American newspaper any day of the week to learn about the devastating effects on the young. Family break-down generates unparented children who attend schools that increasingly resemble detention homes rather than centers of enduring training, discipline, and education and contributes to out-of-wedlock births and violence at unprecedented levels.[2]

## Democracy requires a democratic culture

Democratic theorists historically have either taken for granted a backdrop of vibrant, informal and formal civic associations, or they have articulated explicitly the relationship between democracy and the everyday actions and spirit of a people. Democracy requires laws, constitutions, and authoritative institutions but also depends on democratic dispositions. These include a preparedness to work with others for shared ends, a combination of often strong convictions coupled with a readiness to compromise in the recognition that one can't always get everything one wants, a sense of individuality and a commitment to civic goods that are not the possession of one person or of one small group alone. The world that nourished and sustained such democratic dispositions was a thickly interwoven social fabric—the web of mediating institutions already noted.

Alexis de Tocqueville, in *Democracy in America*, warned of a world different from the robust democracy he surveyed. He urged Americans to take to heart a possible corruption of their way of life. In his worst-case scenario, narrowly self-involved individualists, disarticulated from the saving constraints and nurture of overlapping associations of social life, would require more and more controls "from above" to muffle at least somewhat the disintegrative effects of egoism. To this end, civic spaces between citizens and the state needed to be secured and nourished. Only many small-scale civic bodies would enable citizens to cultivate democratic virtues and to play an active role in the democratic community. Tocqueville's fears were not that anarchy would result but, rather, that new forms of domination might arise. With the disintegration of all social webs, the individual would find himself or herself isolated and impotent, exposed and unprotected. Into this power vacuum would move a centralized, top-heavy state or other centralized and organized forces that would, so to speak, push social life to the lowest common denominator.

---

*Liberal democracy is in trouble in America.*

---

A *New York Times* article on the 1994 campaign reported that "U.S. Voters Focus on Selves, Poll Says." The article raises questions about the long-range impact of such attitudes on the legitimacy and sustainability of liberal democratic institutions. The *Times* noted a "turn inward" and the lack of any "clear direction in the public's political thinking other than frustration with the current system and an eager responsiveness to alternative political solutions and appeals."[3] Based on a *Times-Mirror* survey, the article noted that manifestations of voter frustration included growing disidentification with either of the major parties and massive political rootlessness among the young tethered to high rates of pessimism about the future. Most striking was a significant decline in "public support for social welfare programs," although the level of social tolerance for minorities and homosexuals was high so long as one did not have to bear the burden of financial support or direct "hands-on" involvement in the issue.[4]

## The spiral of delegitimation

Two trends are traceable directly to the collapse of America's social ecology or, alternatively, helped to bring about the negative developments reported in the *Times-Mirror* survey. One is the tendency to remove political disputation from the political arena into the courts. Thus, Americans have witnessed over the past four decades a tendency to derail public debate by judicial fiat. The second is the emergence of a new form of plebiscitary democracy that reduces voters and legislators alike to passive (albeit angry) consumers or instruments. It is not overstating the case to speak of a "spiral of delegitimation" that has its origins in widespread cynicism about government and politics, the disintegration of civil society, a pervasive sense of powerlessness, and other cultural phenomena.

The political scientist James Q. Wilson argues that one reason Americans are more cynical and less trusting than they used to be is that government increasingly has taken on issues that it is ill-equipped to handle well—volatile moral questions such as abortion and "family values," for example. These "wedge issues," as political strategists call them, were generated in part by federal courts who made decisions in the 1960s and 1970s on a whole range of cultural questions without due consideration of how public support for juridically mandated outcomes might be generated. Such juridical moves not only froze out citizen debate but deepened a juridical model of politics, first pushed by liberal activists but now embraced by their conservative counterparts. Juridical politics is "winner take all" built on an adversarial model. This model, in turn, spurs "direct mail" and other mass membership organizations whose primary goal is to give no quarter in any matter of direct interest to them and to them alone. By guaranteeing that the forces on either side of such issues as abortion, or certain highly controversial mandated "remedies" to enforce racial or gender equity, need never debate directly with each other through deliberative processes and legislatures, the courts deepened citizen frustration and fueled a politics of resentment.

In turn, this politics of resentment tends to reduce legislators to passive instruments of single-issue lobbies and media overkill. That is, even as judicial overreach takes issues out of the hands of citizens and legislators, it also appears to be one more factor eroding the deliberative functions of the legislative branch. Take, for example, the continuing American travail over the politics of abortion. One begins with a deeply contentious matter on which people of goodwill are divided. The Supreme Court makes a dramatic preemptive move (*Roe v. Wade*, 1973) that undercuts a nationwide political debate that had grown up from the grass roots. Sixteen states had already moved to make abortion more widely available, and others were poised to take up the question. The Supreme Court's action aroused strong and shocked opposition. The debate turned immediately into a harsh "for" or "against" politics that generated direct-mail, single-issue membership groups who vowed to evaluate representatives on the basis of abortion. But, in a way, this was a desperate strategy as all post-Roe politics had to make its way to the Court, the Court having taken over final prerogative on the question. This model of juridical preemption followed by resentment at the outcome, or fear on the part of those who support it that a mandated outcome may be reversed, frames political questions in a way that places them "beyond compromise."

In the face of such developments, aggrieved citizens say, in effect, "Let's take things back," through direct, rather than representative democracy. Indeed, the *Times-Mirror* survey cited above concluded that the "Perot phenomenon" that speaks to widespread voter anger and resentment went deeper and was more persistent than experts believed. It comes down to this: Judicial fiat displaces institutions of constitutional democracy by radically expanding its own mandate into the realm of democratic debate and compromise where things can be worked out in a rough and ready way. In turn, the proclaimed solution to expanded juridical power, plebiscitary or direct democracy, poses a threat of another (albeit related) sort by promoting the illusion that the unmediated "will of the people" will have final say on all issues. Although we are nowhere close to an official plebiscitary system, the trend is disturbing.

---

*Democracy requires laws, constitutions, and authoritative institutions but also depends on democratic dispositions.*

---

Taken together, the tendency to govern by polls (word has it that the current [Clinton] and several previous administrations bring pollsters to high-level strategy meetings in order to decide what policy should be), the craven capitulation to threats from such mass membership organizations as the American Association of Retired People (AARP) or the National Rifle Association (NRA), and the rise of a very sour populism that feeds on mistrust of government and hatred of politicians—all these excite plebiscitary fervor that deepens the spiral of delegitimation. Currently, those who call themselves populists target anyone unlucky enough to hold government office. Advocates of direct democracy claim that they will perfect democracy by eliminating all barriers between the people's will and its forthright articulation. An elected representative is no longer viewed as someone designated to study and to weigh issues; rather, he or she is to be instructed and to vote predictably based on the demands of single-issue groups and lobbies.

## Plebiscitary democracy

One proposal that surfaced during the Perot candidacy was reminiscent of calls issued as early as the late 1970s for plebiscitary initiatives in the name of promoting democratic citizenship, although, in fact, it undermines the democracy it purports to bolster. I refer to schemes for instant plebiscites via interactive television or telepolling celebrated by their proponents as a technologically more perfect democracy. But plebiscitary majoritarianism is quite different from a democratic polity sustained by debate and judgment. Plebiscites have often sought to shore up antidemocratic regimes—Peronism [under Juan Peron, 1946–1955] in Argentina and Augusto Pinochet in Chile [1974–1990] come to mind. In a plebiscitary system, the views of the majority by definition swamp minority or unpopular views.

Plebiscitarianism is compatible with authoritarian politics carried out under the guise of, or with the connivance of, the ritualistic registering of majority opinion. There is no need for debate with one's fellow citizens on substantive questions. All that is required is a calibration of opinion that, once voiced, solidifies into affirmation or negation of simplistically presented alternatives. Citizens and legislators alike are stripped of the possibility and duty of deliberation and choice. Being asked to proffer an opinion and to register it instantly seems democratic. But he or she expressing an opinion is reduced to a private person by contrast to the public citizen liberal democracy presumes and requires. Tying the 25 percent decline in associational memberships over the past quarter-century to a number of phenomena, Robert Putnam notes that the "most obvious and probably the most powerful instrument of this revolution is television."[5] What televoting would do is to fully legitimate our loss of sociality by making it possible for us to register a political opinion or "taste" as private persons, enclosed within ourselves, rather than as public citizens. To see button-pressing as a meaningful act on a par with lobbying, meeting neighbors, serving on the local school board, working for a candidate, or helping to forge a coalition to promote a particular program or policy parallels a crude version of so-called preference theory in economics.

This theory holds that in a free-market society, the sum total of individual consumer choices results in the greatest benefit to society as a whole even as these choices meet individual "needs." The assumption is that each of us is a "preference maximizer." Aside from being a simplistic account of human motivation, it denies the possibility of social goods—there are only aggregates of private goods. Measuring our opinions through "electronic town halls" is a variant on this crude but common notion. The cure it promises is more of precisely what ails us. Under the banner of more perfected democratic choice, we shall erode even further those elements of deliberation, reason, judgment, and shared goodwill that alone make genuine choice, hence democracy, possible. We would complete the ongoing process of turning our representatives into factotums, mouthpieces expressing our electronically generated "will."

## The future of our democracy

The tale here told traces the unraveling of the institutions of civil society, hence the dramatic upsurge in all forms of social mistrust and generalized fearfulness and cynicism, to the current crisis of governing I have called a spiral of delegitimation. Recent studies show that Americans of all races "cite the same social problems: crime, poor education, imperiled sanctity of home and family."[6] Indeed, if anything, black Americans are more insistent that their society faces a crisis in values, beginning with the family. But there is less agreement on why things have gone wrong and what can be done to put them right. "More economic opportunity" is cited, vaguely but persistently, as a goal for blacks, who also express almost no confidence in American legal institutions or politics, yet want "government" to create jobs and opportunities. Whites see a smaller role for government but not surprisingly, given recent developments, neither whites nor blacks express confidence in the institutions of liberal democratic society. Both groups, in other words, seem ripe for Perot-type "direct democracy" efforts and both seem equally susceptible to the distortion of democratic debate in the hands of media scandalmongers and unscrupulous demagogues. This is a situation begging for a true democratic debate and courageous leadership and wise legislation.

The sociologist Robert Bellah reports that Americans today brighten to tales of community, especially if the talk is soothing and doesn't appear to demand very much from them. Yet when the discussion turns to the need to sustain and to support authoritative civic institutions, attention withers and a certain sourness arises. This bodes ill for liberal democratic society, a political regime that requires robust yet resilient institutions that embody and reflect, yet mediate and shape, the urgencies or democratic passions and interests. As our mediating institutions, from the Parent-Teacher Association to political parties, disappear or are stripped of legitimacy, a political wilderness spreads. People roam the prairie fixing on objects or policies or persons to excoriate or to celebrate, at least for a time until some other enthusiasm or scandal sweeps over them. If we have lost the sturdiness and patience necessary to sustain civil society over the long haul, liberal democracy itself—as a system, a social world, and a culture—is in trouble.

## Notes

1. See, for example, Robert D. Putnam, "Bowling Alone: Democracy in America at the End of the Twentieth Century," which summarizes the empirical data on the sharp and insistent plummeting of civic engagement in the United States. (Unpublished paper, Department of Government, Harvard University, August 1994.) Cited with permission. [Subsequently published as "Bowling Alone: America's Declining Social Capital," *Journal of Democracy*, vol. 6, no. 1, January 1995.]

2. See, for example, Sylvia Ann Hewlett, *When the Bough Breaks: The Cost of Neglecting Our Children* (New York: Basic Books, 1991); and Jean Bethke Elshtain, "Family Matters," *Christian Century*, July 14–21, 1993, 710–711.

3. "U.S. Voters Focus on Selves, Poll Says," *New York Times*, September 21, 1994, A-21.

4. "The People, the Press and Politics: The New Political Landscape," *Times-Mirror* survey, September 21, 1994.

5. Op. cit. Putnam, 25.

6. Gerald F. Seib and Joe Davidson, "Whites, Blacks Agree on Problems; the Issue Is How to Solve Them," *Wall Street Journal*, September 29, 1994, A-1, A-6.

# 2
# Faith in Democratic Society Is Not Declining

## Michael Schudson

*Michael Schudson is a professor of communication and sociology at the University of California, San Diego, and a fellow at the Center for Advanced Study in the Behavioral Sciences. He is the author of several books on the news, popular culture, and politics, including* The Power of News.

Some political and social observers see the decline of voting in America as an indication that Americans are losing faith in democratic civil society. However, the decline of voting and feelings of political ineffectiveness among voters are attributable to the overwhelming demands that the current model of political participation places on voters. American voters can participate effectively in politics simply by voting according to their interests and by holding politicians, political lobbies, and the media accountable.

If recent trends hold up, only about one of every three eligible voters will show up at the polls this fall [1994]. Inevitably, many will conclude that Americans have once again failed as citizens. The problem, however, may not be individual failure so much as our contemporary conception of how democratic citizenship ought to work. Nothing puts that conception into clearer perspective than changes in the act of voting over the past 200 years.

## Voting rites in American history

Imagine yourself a voter in the world of colonial Virginia where George Washington, Patrick Henry, and Thomas Jefferson learned their politics. As a matter of law, you must be a white male owning at least a modest amount of property. Your journey to vote may take several hours since there is probably only one polling place in the county. As you approach the courthouse, you see the sheriff supervising the election. Two candidates for office stand before you, both of them members of prominent local families. You watch the most prominent members of the community,

Michael Schudson, "Voting Rites: Why We Need a New Concept of Citizenship," *American Prospect*, Fall 1994; © 1994, New Prospect, Inc. Reprinted with permission of the *American Prospect*.

the leading landowner and clergyman, cast their votes, and you know whom they have supported because they announce their votes in loud, clear voices. You do the same and then step over to the candidate for whom you have voted, and he treats you to a glass of rum punch. Your vote has been an act of restating and reaffirming the social hierarchy of a community where no one but a local notable would think of standing for office.

Now imagine you are in eighteenth-century Massachusetts rather than Virginia. The model of voting is different, as you elect town select-men and representatives at a town meeting. But, like Virginia, the New England model reflects an organic view that the polity has a single common good and that the leaders of locally prominent, wealthy, and well-established families can be trusted to represent it. Dissent and conflict are no more acceptable in New England than in Virginia.

Move the clock ahead to the nineteenth century, as mass political parties cultivate a new democratic order. Now there is much more bustle around the polling place. The area is crowded with the banners and torches of rival parties. Election day is not set off from other days but is the culmination of a campaign of several months. You must still be a white male but not necessarily of property. During the campaign, you have marched in torchlight processions in military uniform with a club of like-minded men from your party. They may accompany you to the polls. If you were not active in the campaign, you may be roused on election day by a party worker to escort you on foot or by carriage. On the road, you may encounter clubs or groups from rival parties, and it would not be unusual if fisticuffs or even guns were to dissuade you from casting a ballot after all.

If you do proceed to the ballot box, you may step more lively with the encouragement of a dollar or two from the party—less a bribe than an acknowledgment that voting is a service to your party. A party worker hands you a colored ballot with the printed names of the party's candidates. You may also receive a slightly smaller ballot with the same names on it that can be surreptitiously placed inside the other so that you can cast two ballots rather than one. You are willing to do so not out of a strong sense that your party offers better public policies but because your party is your party, just as, in our own day, your high school is your high school. In any event, parties tend to be more devoted to distributing offices than to advocating policies.

*Whatever else we learn from elections, we are tutored in a sense of helplessness and fundamental inadequacy to the task of citizenship.*

Now turn to the early twentieth century as Progressive era reforms cleanse voting of what made it both compelling and, by our standards, corrupt. Reformers find the emphasis in campaigns on spectacle rather than substance much too emotional. They pioneer what they term an "educational campaign" that stresses the distribution of pamphlets on the issues rather than parades of solidarity. They pass legislation to ensure a secret ballot. They enact voter registration statutes. They help create an atmosphere in which it becomes more common for traditionally loyal party newspapers to "bolt" from party-endorsed candidates. They insist on official state ballots rather than party ballots and in some states develop state-approved voter information booklets rather than leaving education up to the parties themselves. At the same time, civil service reform limits the rewards parties can distribute to loyal partisans.

## Voting today

The world we experience today at the polls has been handed down to us from these reforms. What does voting look like and feel like today?

I asked my students at the University of California, San Diego, to write about their experience of voting in 1992. Many of them had never voted before; hardly any had voted in a presidential election. It is something they looked forward to doing, especially those who supported Clinton. Still, some students felt a letdown in the act of voting:

> As I punched in the holes on my voting card, a slight sense of disappointment clouded my otherwise cheerful mood. First of all, the building behind Revelle Bargain Books was not what I had always imagined as a polling place. How could a location this close to the all-you-can-eat cafeteria be the site of a vote to choose the leader of our nation? Second, I could not understand why there were no curtains around my booth. As a child I can always remember crawling under curtains in voting booths to spy on my parents. Why couldn't I have those curtains to hide all of my important, private decisions?

Or listen to this student, a Filipino-American who voted for Bush:

> The more I tried to be aware of the political goings-on, through television mainly, the more I became aggravated with the whole situation. Perot represented the evil of a one-man monopoly, while Clinton was a man who knew how to manipulate an audience and use the media. In addition, Hillary reminded me of the stories and comments my parents made about Imelda Marcos. Taxes came to mind every time I considered Bush, but I decided he might be the best qualified candidate.

> My Dad was an influential part of my decision to go; not because he urged me to do so, but so that after the election I would finally be able to tell him that I voted.

> Needless to say, no one at the polling site seemed to talk politics, at least not when I was there. The silence did not bother me, though, since I am definitely not confident enough to talk politics to anyone outside of my family!

Or this immigrant Russian:

> My Mom went to vote with me that day (at the polling place in a neighbor's garage). The night before, I had marked my mother's sample ballot with circles around "yes" and "no" on particular propositions and checked the boxes next to "Feinstein" and "Boxer" so she would not forget. The sample ballot is very convenient. The propositions are especially grueling to read. They disguise themselves in legal/state jargon and refuse to give way to meaning.

I felt distantly connected to other voters in other garages who would be making the same vote for change as I would. Nevertheless, I went through my ballot, standing in that cardboard cubicle, in a very ordinary way, feeling that I was, most likely, insignificant and that my views would find no representation. I remember guessing on some local offices, like county supervisor, and trying not to pick a "Christian right" candidate.

The individuality and jealously guarded privacy of voting today contrasts dramatically with the *viva voce* process of eighteenth-century Virginia or the colorful party ticket voting of the nineteenth century. So do the indecision and uncertainty. The students felt inadequate to the election—and why not? The list of propositions and complex voter information pamphlet in California were overwhelming. My voter information pamphlet for the June 1994 primary ran forty-eight pages—and that was just for city and county offices and referenda. For state offices and ballot measures, a separate publication ran sixty-four pages. The obscurity of many candidates and issues encouraged mass pre-election mailings of leaflet slates of candidates produced by profit-making organizations with no connection to political parties. I received, for instance, *Voter Information Guide for Democrats* and *Crime Fighters '94* produced by "Democratic Choice '94." The weary voter had to read the fine print to learn that neither slate was endorsed by the Democratic party.

Whatever else we learn from elections, we are tutored in a sense of helplessness and fundamental inadequacy to the task of citizenship. We are told to be informed but discover that the information required to cast an informed vote is beyond our capacities. We are reminded that the United States has the lowest voter turnout of any democracy but rarely told that we have more elections for more levels of government with more elective offices at each level than any other country in the world. We are enjoined by critics of Lockean liberalism to devote ourselves more heartily to the public weal as social beings, but in the primal act of citizenship we face the ballot alone, in privacy, with our own conscience, face to face with our own ignorance.

## The burden of Progressivism

We need a new concept of citizenship, one that asks something from us but is not burdened with the impossible expectations of the Progressive model. Contrast what we implicitly expect of ourselves today and what Thomas Jefferson hoped for citizens 200 years ago. In the preamble of Bill 79 to establish universal elementary instruction in Virginia, Jefferson observed that the people normally elect men of standing in the community. The community needs especially to educate these leaders. As for the citizenry at large, Jefferson sought to inculcate through the study of history knowledge that "they may be enabled to know ambition under all its shapes, and prompt to exert their natural powers to defeat its purposes." That was the whole of the citizen's job—watchfulness to defeat ambition.

Citizens were decidedly not to undertake their own evaluation of issues before the legislature. That was the job of representatives. The Founding Fathers assumed that voters would and should choose representatives on the basis of character, not issues. Representatives would have enough in common with the people they represented to keep their "interests" in mind. For the Founding Fathers, elected representatives—not parties, not interest groups, not newspapers, not citizens in the streets—were to make policy.

We have come to ask more of citizens. Today's dominant views about citizenship come from the Progressives' rationalist and ardently individualist worldview. The Progressive impulse was educational—to bring science to politics and professional management to cities, to substitute pamphlets for parades and parlors for streets. The practice of citizenship, at least in campaigning and voting, became privatized, more effortful, more cognitive, and a lot less fun.

In the eighteenth and nineteenth centuries, there was no concern about the people who did not vote. Political science and public discourse began to worry about nonvoters only after World War I when voting rates had declined to a low not reached again until the 1970s. The National Association of Manufacturers, the news media, and other groups responded by designing "get out the vote" campaigns, those largely fruitless moral injunctions to "vote, vote for whomever you choose, but vote." Such slogans were unheard-of in the decades of highest voter turnout from 1840 to 1900. You sure as hell did not want people from the other party voting. Campaigns were military efforts. You already knew who stood in your army behind your banner; the task of the campaign was to get them to the polls. Citizenship was social; the Progressives, in the name of rationality and education, changed all that.

The Progressive ideal requires citizens to possess a huge fund of political information and a ceaseless attentiveness to public issues. This could never be. Even at the Constitutional Convention of 1787 a delegate observed that people grew "listless" with frequent elections. Fifty years later Alexis de Tocqueville lamented, "Even when one has won the confidence of a democratic nation, it is a hard matter to attract its attention." A half century thereafter Woodrow Wilson wrote:

> The ordinary citizen cannot be induced to pay much heed to the details unless something else more interesting than the law itself be involved. . . . If the fortunes of a party or the power of a great political leader are staked upon the final vote, he will listen with the keenest interest . . . but if no such things hang in the balance, he will not turn from his business to listen.

So if, as some people suggest these days, Americans suffer from a political attention deficit disorder, it has been incubating for a long time. Perhaps television or party decline exacerbates it. But public inattention has been a fact of political life, with only momentary escapes, through our history. If this is so, what is a reasonable expectation for citizens, a reasonable standard of citizen competence?

## A practical citizenship

Under democratic government, as the Founding Fathers constituted it, the representatives of the people could carry on the business of governing without individual citizens' becoming experts on the questions of policy placed before the Congress. Similarly, technologies of cognition, as Donald Norman argues in his book *Things That Make Us Smart*, allow us to act more intelligently without being any smarter or performing great feats of memory. We can carry a datebook, consult a dictionary, use a calculator, run spell check. We don't have to keep everything in our heads. Cognition is distributed.

Citizens are not to be created one by one, pouring into each of them enough newspapers, information, or virtuous resolve for them to judge each issue and each candidate rationally. That is where the Progressive vision went wrong. Citizens flourish in an environment that supports worthwhile citizenship activities. We should be intent on creating such an environment, not on turning every voter into an expert.

---

*[People] make intelligent voting decisions based only in small measure on their attending to campaign issues.*

---

If, like the Progressives, we take citizenship to be a function of the individual, we are bound to be discouraged. A classical model of citizenship asks that people seek the good of the general, the public. But this is either utopian—people just do not pay that kind of attention—or else undesirable because it honors public life to the exclusion of workaday labor or inner spiritual pursuits. A more Lockean, modern, realistic version is that citizens should be moved in public life by self-interest and so should acquire a fair understanding of their own interests and which public policies best serve them. But people's knowledge of public affairs fails even by this standard. Even self-interest in politics is a surprisingly weak reed since the gratifications of private life—getting home on time rather than stopping at the polls to vote, spending seven or eight dollars for a movie rather than for a campaign contribution—are more visible and immediate than the marginal contribution one might make to determining policy by voting, signing a petition, or writing a letter.

How low can we go? We can seek to build a political system where individuals will perform the right actions for their own or the public's interest without knowing much at all. People will do the right thing in general ignorance. User-friendly technology works this way; almost anyone can drive a car while knowing scarcely anything about what makes it run.

In *The Reasoning Voter*, Samuel Popkin suggests we are pretty close to this user-friendly politics already. Relatively little of what voters know, Popkin argues, comes to them as abstract political intelligence. They make intelligent voting decisions based only in small measure on their attending to campaign issues. People have little of the propositional knowledge that models of citizenship demand, but they have more background knowledge than they may realize. They know about economic issues because they have savings accounts, home mortgages, or mutual funds. They have views about health care reform because they know someone personally who has been denied health insurance because of a preexisting condition. They have enough "by-product information" from daily life to make the broad, either-or choice of a presidential candidate in ways consistent with their own interests and views. Even in presidential primaries, Popkin suggests, shifts in voter allegiance are better explained by a model of "low-information rationality" than by media manipulation or passions run riot.

In elections for school boards and other local contests, however, where public information about candidates is more limited and there are often no party labels (again, thanks to Progressive reforms), voters may find themselves in the polling booth without a clue about whom to support. This is not a new condition, if the humorist Finley Peter Dunne (1867–1936) is to be believed: "A rayformer thinks he was ilicted because he was a rayformer, whin th' thruth iv th' matther is he was ilicted because no wan knew him."

## The citizens' trustees

Citizens have to find trustees for their citizenship. Identifying adequate trustees and holding them responsible, I submit, is where we should focus attention. There are three main sets of trustees: politicians, lobbyists, and journalists. Elected officials are our primary trustees. Their obligation is to act with the public in view. They act not so much in response to deliberative public opinion—which rarely exists—but in anticipation of future reward or punishment at the polls. The politicians may not always perceive public opinion accurately. They may not judge well just how much they can lead and shape and how much they must follow and bow to public sentiment. But the motivational structure of elective office demands that they must always be sensitive on this point.

Lobbyists are a second set of trustees. If you believe in the individual's right to bear arms unrestrained by federal legislation, send your annual dues to the National Rifle Association. If you believe that the environment needs aggressive protection, send your dues to an environmental action group. If you do not know what you believe—and this is the common condition for most people on most issues before the nation—you will do better at expressing your will if you at least know that you tend to favor one party over another. Partisanship is a still-useful cue. The rise of the "independent" voter has been much exaggerated, political scientists have now come to see, and party loyalty remains meaningful. Even in the American system where parties tend to converge on a middle ground, they arrive there from different directions and, in a pinch, fall back on contrasting inclinations.

Two mechanisms keep politician-trustees responsible. The first is the election, fallible as it is. If the representative does not satisfy the citizens, they have a regularly scheduled opportunity to throw the bum out. The second constraint on the politician is the party system. Of course, the party is a more effective discipline on wayward politicians in strong parliamentary systems than in the United States. Here parties are relatively weak, and entrepreneurial politicians relatively independent of them. Still, a politician's party affiliation is a check on his or her policy views and a useful piece of information for voters.

The demands citizens make on lobbyists are much narrower than those placed on politicians—lobbyists are expected to be advocates rather than judges, suppliers of information and resources to sympathetic politicians rather than builders of politically viable solutions to public problems. They are the instructed agents of their organizations rather than Burkean independent-minded representatives. As individuals, they are easy to hold responsible. The question of responsibility with lobbyists is how to hold the whole system responsible since the balance of lobbying power tilts heavily toward the richest and most powerful groups in society. If the system works, it facilitates expression for intensely felt interests from the far corners of the country; if it works badly, it twists and clogs up the primary system of political representation.

The usual answer is to seek to limit the influence of lobbies through campaign finance reform and other restrictions on lobbying activities. An alternative approach seeks to grant lobbyists more authority rather than less influence. Instead of closing down access where the rich and powerful have the resources to guarantee their over-representation, can entree be opened in settings where a broad array of interest groups are assured a voice? In decision making in some federal administrative agencies, interest groups have been granted quasi-public standing. The Negotiated Rulemaking Act of 1990 enables agencies like the Environmental Protection Agency (EPA) and the Occupational Safety and Health Administration to create committees of private organizations to write regulatory rules.

For instance, EPA arranged for the Sierra Club and the Natural Resources Defense Council to sit down with the American Petroleum Institute and the National Petroleum Refiners Association to work out rules to carry out the Clean Air Act. Millions of Americans belong to organizations that employ paid lobbyists; the lobbies are not about to disappear nor should they. But controlling them may be a delicate balance of restraining some kinds of influence while orchestrating other public opportunities for special interests to take on responsibility for governing.

The third set of trustees—the media—is the most difficult to hold accountable. The market mechanism does not serve well here. People buy a newspaper or watch a television network for many purposes besides gathering political information. The quality or quantity of political intelligence does not correlate well with the rise and fall of newspaper circulations or television news ratings.

---

*If the representative does not satisfy the citizens, they have a regularly scheduled opportunity to throw the bum out.*

---

There are, as the French press critic Claude-Jean Bertrand suggests, a variety of "media accountability systems"—nongovernmental mechanisms to keep the news media responsible to public interests and opinions. These include codes of ethics, in-house critics, media reporters, and ombudsmen, as well as liaison committees that news institutions have sometimes established with social groups they may report on or clash with. There are also letters to the editor, journalism reviews, journalism schools, awards for good news coverage, and libel suits or the threat of libel.

But media criticism is in crisis. There is little agreement on what the media should be doing. Increasingly critics charge that providing information is not enough; they say that providing so much information with so little direction on how to interpret it may confuse and alienate the audience. These critics urge that journalists have an obligation to engage, not just to inform. But others respond that this goes beyond the appropriate role for the press. They say that muckraking may make the blood boil momentarily, but will more likely teach cynicism than activism.

Still others have urged the media both to resist the agenda of politicians and to refrain from imposing their own. Instead, these critics, such as Jay Rosen of New York University, recommend a "public journalism" in which the press actively solicits public views through surveys, focus groups, town meetings, and other mechanisms to arrive at a "public agenda" that the news media can then take as a brief for news coverage. This is a novel direction that some news organizations have responded to with enthusiasm. And it is a hopeful sign that at least some editors and publishers feel an urgency about reconceiving themselves and committing themselves to making democratic citizenship possible.

Other experiments are taking place, too. In cities where government has established decentralized neighborhood councils, the councils may run their own newspapers or have assured space for their proceedings and announcements in freely distributed commercial papers—as in St. Paul, Minnesota. Still, there is no consensus today on just what standards for the press are appropriate.

## The overworked citizen

William James said nearly a century ago that our moral destiny turns on "the power of voluntarily attending." But, he added, though crucial to our individual and collective destinies, attention tends to be "brief and fitful." This is the substantial underlying reality of political life that any efforts at enlarging citizenship must confront. Can we have a democracy if most people are not paying attention most of the time? The answer is that this is the only kind of democracy we will ever have. Our ways of organizing and evoking that brief and fitful attention are different but not necessarily any worse from those in our past.

One response could be to harness the rare moments of attentiveness. Social movements and the occasional closely fought, morally urgent election have sometimes done that. When political scientists have looked at intensively fought senatorial campaigns, for instance, and compared them to run-of-the-mill campaigns, they find much more information in the news media about candidates' policy positions, increased knowledge among voters about those positions, and apparently increased inclination of voters to make decisions on the issues. At the level of presidential politics and occasionally in senatorial or gubernatorial politics, there is enough information available for voter rationality to have a chance; but for other offices, Alan Ehrenhalt may be right in his book *The United States of Ambition* that our elections say much more about the supply of candidates than the demands of voters.

An alternate response would be to build a society that makes more of situations that build citizenship without taxing attentiveness. In an environment that supports worthwhile citizenship activity, there is intrinsic reward for doing the right thing. If we interpret citizenship activity to mean taking unpaid and uncoerced responsibility for the welfare of strangers or the community at large, examples of good citizenship abound. I think of the people who serve as "room parents" in the schools or coach Little League. Why do they do it? Their own children would do just as well if someone else took on the job. Coaching Little League or serving in the Parent-Teachers Association are activities or practices rather than cognitive efforts; they are social and integrated into community life. They make citizenship itself into a "by-product" effect. Their success suggests that citizenship may be harder to instill when it involves burdens beyond daily life than to engineer it as an everyday social activity. The volunteers may not enjoy every minute, but they find intrinsic social reward in having friends, neighbors, and strangers praise and admire them.

Our common language for a better public life seems impoverished. We think of politicians with distrust rather than thinking of ways to enforce their trustworthiness. We think of lobbyists with disdain instead of thinking of ways to recognize and harness their virtues. We think of journalists alternately as heroes or scoundrels. And we think of our own citizenship too often with either guilt at our ignorance and lack of participation or with a moral pat on the back for having sacrificed more than our neighbors. We must think more about building a democratic environment that will make us smarter as a people than we are as individuals.

# 3

# Making Registration Easier Will Increase Voter Turnout

## Jordan Moss

*Jordan Moss is a freelance writer and activist who worked at Human SERVE, a lobbying group for low-income voter registration, from 1988 to 1992.*

The ten-year campaign to pass the National Voter Registration Act of 1993 (the "Motor Voter" law) provides insight into the way regulations on voter registration keep many Americans from voting. The original goal of the campaign was the adoption of a law that would allow low-income citizens (who constitute the majority of nonvoters) to register to vote at welfare and unemployment agencies. Both the Republican and Democratic national parties resisted this strategy because the incorporation of so many new low-income voters would have upset the political status quo. The law that finally passed is intended to promote universal registration, which common sense and existing programs in various states demonstrate will raise voter turnout.

In the early 1980s, noted social scientists and activists Richard Cloward and Frances Fox Piven began work on a strategy aimed to counter Ronald Reagan's relentless attack on the welfare state. Announced in the Winter 1983 issue of *Social Policy*,[1] their plan rested on the premise that by registering massive numbers of poor and low-income people to vote, a strong voting bloc would emerge to stanch the conservative tide and force the Democratic party to move to its left.

Ten years later, Piven and Cloward stood behind President Clinton on May 20, 1993, as he signed the National Voter Registration Act—the "Motor Voter" bill—into law. When it takes effect on January 1, 1995, Americans will be offered the opportunity to register to vote when they apply for government services, including welfare and driver's licenses. Currently, with voter participation levels at a scandalous low (only about 50 percent of eligible voters turn out for presidential elections), fully 70 million people—almost two-fifths of the eligible electorate—are not even

Jordan Moss, "Motor Voter: From Movement to Legislation," *Social Policy*, Winter 1993; © 1993 by Social Policy Corporation. Reprinted with permission.

registered to vote. If the act is implemented correctly, the US will no longer be the only western democracy without a system of universal enfranchisement.

Though a crowning achievement to a decade's work—and arguably the largest advance for voting rights in thirty years—universal voter registration was not what Piven and Cloward had in mind in 1983. At that time, their intention was to register poor and low-income Americans—who comprise two-thirds of the disenfranchised—and thereby politicize a logical constituency to fight the Reagan onslaught on social welfare programs. In the same year they wrote the article, Piven and Cloward formed a nonprofit voter registration reform organization known as Human SERVE (Human Service Employees Voter Registration and Education), whose intent was to register poor people through nonprofit human service agencies.

In the process of advancing various versions of their strategy of agency-based voter registration, however, it became apparent that the poor could not be registered in sufficient numbers to make a difference without totally transforming the country's archaic voter registration apparatus. The events that followed led Piven and Cloward to shift gears, advancing a universal registration strategy that Congress eventually wrote into law. The history of "motor voter," with its intertwining relation to grassroots movements, partisan politics, and lobbying at the state and federal levels, is an object lesson in the long, hard road from theory to practice.

## The original plan

The human service agency strategy pioneered by Human SERVE was predicated on the logic that recipients of social services are a natural constituency for political support of funding to social programs. The best way to reach these recipients, Human SERVE concluded, was through human service workers: they are impersonal contact with service beneficiaries, are often political supporters of human service programs, and have a vested interest in assuring adequate funding to them since their jobs often depend on it.

"In tens of millions of everyday transactions," Piven and Cloward argued in their 1983 article, social service workers could "warn clients about the social program cuts, and they [could] distribute registration forms while making issue-oriented but nonpartisan appeals about the importance of registering and voting. Because of the sheer growth of the welfare state . . . human service workers—more than any other group—now have the capacity to set forces in motion leading to a class-based political realignment."

In its early days, Piven and Cloward predicted the result of Human SERVE's work would be the emergence of a movement with a politically empowered human service constituency at its core. When this movement started making demands on the Democratic party that it could not easily handle, they argued, a significant political realignment in this country would be the result. This movement, they further argued, would gain steam as it confronted the elites that would inevitably try to quash attempts to facilitate the registration of poor people. "If elites clamp down on the exercise of political rights in reaction to a registration movement, they will reveal that the interests of business and industry depend upon excluding the poor and minorities from the political system."

---

*With voter participation levels at a scandalous low, . . . fully 70 million people—almost two-fifths of the eligible electorate—are not even registered to vote.*

---

As we now know, a movement of this kind never developed. Voter registration was a logical tool (it had sparked a major movement in the 1960s, after all), and Human SERVE did enlist the support of the leadership of important voluntary agencies such as Planned Parenthood and the YWCA, public employee unions, and professional social work associations—all of whom welcomed the strategy and vowed to implement it. But the politically fragile nature of human service work and the sheer number of agencies involved severely inhibited the implementation of effective programs. Most importantly, agency directors feared that voter registration "would provoke the wrath either of their rich and conservative board members or of incumbent political leaders who dispense public subsidies."[2]

## A change in direction

In terms of Piven and Cloward's original goals the voluntary agency strategy failed. "By the close of registration in 1984, 1,500 voluntary agencies across the country had registered 275,000 people. . . . Still, this had to be seen as a modest result. Voluntary agencies have the capacity to register millions, but only about one percent of them participated," Piven and Cloward wrote in 1985.[3]

This lesson was compounded by the experience of the massive voter registration drive in which Human SERVE participated in 1984. While the work of a broad range of nonpartisan groups—among them Project VOTE, Citizen Action, and ACORN in addition to Human SERVE—registered a few million people, many of them from traditional Democratic constituencies, the Democratic National Committee did virtually nothing to help the effort.

The Republicans, in the meantime, weren't taking any chances. GOP strategists and Christian Right activists took seriously the threat that the Democratic party might expand the electorate from the bottom, and mounted a massive high-tech voter registration campaign utilizing data tapes from the Census Bureau, credit bureaus, motor vehicle bureaus, financial magazines, upscale mail-order houses and boards of registrars to target unregistered but likely Republican voters.[4] As Piven and Cloward put it, the registration wars of 1984 ended in a "class stalemate," partly because the nonpartisan groups didn't all target low-income populations, and partly because of the counterbalancing effects of successful Republican registration among wealthier constituencies.[5] In the wake of the 1984 elections, expecting future such efforts to be as futile, Human SERVE changed its strategy.

At the same time, Human SERVE was beginning to understand what it was up against. Its campaigns to register voters were waged in the context of a labyrinthine registration system put into place at the end of the 19th century purposely to disenfranchise working-class voters. Fearful of a growing and unpredictable electorate, and of fraud—both real and imagined—politicians imposed registration and residency requirements under the guise of good-government reform. Turnout declined precipitously as a result.

The one unfortunate legacy of the Voting Rights Act of 1964 is that it has convinced almost everyone that once poll taxes and literacy tests were abolished, voter registration had been made easy. But equally effective, if somewhat more subtle, income and education tests were and are still prevalent. Many jurisdictions require people to travel to a county seat during working hours to register, increasing the difficulty of registration for working people. Some states such as Illinois and Massachusetts require those wishing to register others to be deputized, leaving it to local boards of elections to decide who should be granted this privilege. Notarization and witness requirements hobble the path to the franchise in other states. And mail-in registration currently is permitted in only half of the states, and where it is allowed forms are not made widely available the way income tax and selective service registration forms are. (While states may differ slightly in how they will register voters at state agencies, all of these burdensome requirements are prohibited by the new law. In addition, mail-in registration will also be required in all states.)

All of this complicated, and in many cases legally prevented, Human SERVE's attempts to establish voter registration programs in human service agencies. Confronting these institutionalized barriers repeatedly during extensive experience in the field, Human SERVE turned its efforts to promoting institutional reform in public agencies, focusing almost all of its attention there by the mid-1980s. The shift represented an important change in direction: from mobilization of the social service sector to advocating universal voter registration with elected and public officials. Both strategies, however, shared the goal of gaining political power for the chronically underrepresented.

## Gaining support

Anticipating the resistance of the national parties and incumbent legislatures to expanding the electorate, Human SERVE and its regional organizers capitalized on the fragmentary nature of American government and convinced sympathetic governors (particularly liberal Democrats like Mario Cuomo in New York and Richard Celeste in Ohio, who had won office in 1982 as a result of a huge surge in voter participation among the poor), mayors, and county officials to issue executive orders mandating that workers in a variety of government agencies—including but not exclusive to welfare and unemployment offices—offer applicants for services assistance in completing voter registration forms. The strategy was buttressed by endorsements from the National Association of Secretaries of State, the National League of Cities and coalition support from labor unions and scores of other national human service organizations. Human SERVE hoped that by significantly raising registration levels, members of Congress would have little reason *not* to ratify, through federal legislation, what was already occurring in their home states.

But this strategy, although successful in many localities, also never reached critical mass. While the fragmentary nature of the American polity allowed Human SERVE to bypass the legislatures and score scattered victories through executive branch actions, the size of the country and its infinite jurisdictions militated against achieving truly wide-scale expansion in voter rolls. Also, the gubernatorial executive orders—which held significant promise, with many of them issued in the most populous states (Texas, Ohio, New York)—were, in effect, rendered impotent by a hostile Reagan Administration, which threatened to cut off grants-in-aid to states that used any portion of these federal funds to pay the salary of employees engaged in registration activities. In response, the governors made registration forms available on tables in waiting rooms, but did not instruct employees to assist in filling them out. As has been found repeatedly, such "passive" efforts yield few new registrants.

---

*Campaigns to register voters were waged in the context of a labyrinthine registration system put into place at the end of the 19th century purposely to disenfranchise working-class voters.*

---

The concept of agency-based voter registration was nonetheless gaining momentum and legitimacy with every endorsement, executive order and implemented program. And as the reform front fully advanced to the state level, Human SERVE put to good use its expertise in designing and implementing effective agency-based programs. Ironically, a number of state legislatures, mostly those with Democratic majorities, picked up the concept of agency-based voter registration and began passing what came to be known as "motor voter" measures. "Motor voter" was a concept pioneered by Michigan Secretary of State Richard Austin in 1975. With voter registration and driver's license applications under his purview, he combined the two into a single transaction, allowing people to register to vote when getting a driver's license. While Human SERVE was initially wary of "motor voter" measures because of a perceived upper-income skew among license applicants, and promoted it only to make registration in public assistance agencies more palatable to elected officials, the group eventually realized that the numbers were on their side. Ninety percent of voting age citizens have driver's licenses or personal identification cards issued by motor vehicle bureaus.

### The bill we won

What made Congress, heretofore loathe to expanding the electorate, enact a system of universal voter registration? After all, as Jimmy Carter pointed out after his election-day-registration bill was blocked by Congress, incumbent politicians on both sides of the aisle have little incentive to change the rules of an electoral game that they have already won.

When the "motor voter" bill came to a vote, Democrats overwhelmingly supported it, and Republicans largely opposed it. But registration reform would never have come onto the legislative agenda at all without outside pressure. In 1987, Human SERVE persuaded a Washington coalition of good-government and civil-rights groups to press Congress to support an agency-based initiative, and several versions of "motor voter" were introduced over the next six years. In that time, cost-effective and fraud-free "motor voter" programs in the states proliferated, lending a legitimacy to the concept that has largely eluded election-day registration.

In order to end a Republican filibuster in the Senate, some compromises were made in the "motor voter" bill. The requirement for registration at unemployment offices was dropped, in order to preserve registration at welfare agencies. But, because people in unemployment lines (who generally are part of the stable work force) are likely to be registered in motor vehicle bureaus, the exclusion of unemployment offices from the bill was regarded as a not-too-terrible price to pay. The new law allows states some discretion in implementation, but the bottom line is that they will be required to simultaneously offer applicants for services the opportunity to register to vote.

How effective the new law will be in achieving truly universal registration depends to a great extent on its implementation. Human SERVE is now providing technical assistance to states that are starting to design programs to comply with the federal bill. But the group urges activists to remain vigilant as entrenched state legislatures may balk at fully including the welfare agencies when they draft legislation to execute the federal mandate.

## Will it make a difference?

With effective implementation, tens of millions of previously excluded Americans will be registered to vote as a result of the National Voter Registration Act of 1993. Why, then, has there been so little excitement about the bill?

Many progressives have little faith that new registrants will vote just because they're registered. And if they do vote, the argument goes, they probably won't vote their interests to support progressive politicians, especially with so little variety to choose from. Of course, only time will tell, but I think there is reason for a more optimistic view of both questions.

Although the number of eligible voters who turn out for presidential elections is now down to only about half the population, the figure for *registered* Americans is much higher—as high as 85 percent or more. If all Americans were automatically registered, would we see massive jumps in the number of voters in upcoming elections? Political scientists generally agree that, at least initially, new registrants won't turn out at the same rate as previously registered voters. People who actively choose to go through the process required to register, of course, are expected to turn out in larger numbers than those more or less automatically registered under the motor voter program. But even the most cautious estimates of the effects of universal registration—Ray Wolfinger and Steven Rosenstone estimate that liberalization of voter registration laws will increase turnout by 9.1 percentage points[6]—spell millions of new voters. The success of motor voter programs in the states bolsters arguments that removing barriers to registration significantly lifts turnout. While a variety of economic and political trends led to generally higher voter turnout in

1992 than in 1988, it is important to note that those states with recently implemented motor voter programs experienced increases in registration *and* turnout well above the national average in 1992.[7]

The argument that even if poor people do vote, they probably won't vote their own interest is another often cited ground for skepticism about how much the motor voter bill will change the political landscape. This view, grounded in considerable cynicism, is primarily based on poll data showing that nonvoters would largely support the same candidates as current voters do. If they did vote, in other words it wouldn't make any difference.

---

*The success of motor voter programs in the states bolsters arguments that removing barriers to registration significantly lifts turnout.*

---

While the polls may be accurate, they do not tell what would happen if nonvoters were active players in the election rather than bystanders looking on from the sidelines. Would new political actors emerge to take advantage of a newly empowered constituency? Would traditional leaders try to woo their votes by speaking to their concerns?

Piven and Cloward provided one answer in a 1985 article in the *Nation*. "[V]oting percentages and attitudes would change," they argued, "if leaders bid for the allegiance of new voters from the bottom by articulating their grievances and aspirations. Constituents can influence leaders, and vice versa—as Jesse Jackson's [1984] campaign reminded us. Even Walter Mondale would have run a different campaign [in 1984] if he had been forced to contend with millions of new voters from the bottom."[8]

Water-tight proof that this would be the case is hard to come by, but supporting evidence is found in the election of the progressive Senator Paul Wellstone. Wellstone partly credits his election to Minnesota's model system of agency-based voter registration (a reform his activism helped realize), which is responsible for Minnesota's top ranking among states in voter turnout.

What else would change? The third party efforts currently afoot also stand to gain from broader-based registration and turnout, as they will now be able to compete with the major parties for the allegiances of millions of new voters. And a significant amount of energy will simultaneously be freed to take advantage of the situation, since the time and money these grassroots groups previously spent on voter registration can now presumably be devoted to other work.

But even the most ardent backers of the legislation agree that it is not a panacea. Campaign finance reform is one other important factor in levelling the playing field, and there are more.

Piven and Cloward stress the complementary power of protest movements in exacting concessions from political elites, as is reflected in their initial strategy. Existing electoral coalitions are not strong—some indication of the extent of their fragility is seen in the sudden success of Ross Perot in 1992. With presidential elections often decided by no more than a few million votes, several million new participants sympathetic to progressive movements for social change will add to the instability of those coalitions, potentially forcing a major political realignment. And while it may seem unlikely that a new political constituency will gain an electoral majority, the current political parties, faced with hemorrhaging electoral bases, may at that point be compelled to respond to the movement's demands if they are to hold onto political power. The scenario would not be unprecedented: the southern voting rights movement exacted concessions from the Democratic party thirty years ago [in 1964] in just such a manner.

Whatever happens, the full enfranchisement of the American electorate is at least an election cycle or two away—it will take time for the agencies to reach everyone. But some initial rumblings along these lines may be heard in 1996 if President Clinton's narrow electoral plurality is threatened with defections to his Republican challenger or to Ross Perot. And if it is, New Democrat Clinton may be forced to make concessions to even newer Democrats if he wants to remain in office.

## *Notes*

1. Frances Fox Piven and Richard A. Cloward, "Toward a Class-Based Realignment of American Politics," *Social Policy* (Winter 1983), pp. 3–14.

2. Frances Fox Piven and Richard A. Cloward, "Prospects for Voter Registration Reform: A Report on the Experience of the Human SERVE Campaign," *PS* (Summer 1985), p. 584.

3. Ibid.

4. Frances Fox Piven and Richard A. Cloward, *Why Americans Don't Vote* (New York: Pantheon, 1988), p. 190.

5. Frances Fox Piven and Richard A. Cloward, "Trying to Break Down the Barriers," *Nation* (November 2, 1985), p. 435.

6. Raymond E. Wolfinger and Steven J. Rosenstone, *Who Votes?* (New Haven: Yale University Press, 1980), p. 73.

7. Human SERVE, *News on Agency-Based Voter Registration* (December 1, 1992), p. 6.

8. Frances Fox Piven and Richard A. Cloward, "How to Get Out the Vote in 1988," *Nation* (November 23, 1985).

# 4

# Easier Registration Will Not Significantly Increase Voter Turnout

## Seymour Martin Lipset

*Seymour Martin Lipset is the Hazel Professor of Public Policy at George Mason University in Fairfax, Virginia, and the author of numerous books on political science, sociology, and public policy, including the forthcoming* American Exceptionalism: A Double-Edged Sword.

Since the 1960s, reforms have been enacted to make voter registration easier, yet voting participation has fallen off. This decline has occurred because many Americans believe that their one vote will not make a difference in elections. In addition, most Americans—in contrast to citizens of other democracies—do not respond to arguments that voting is a moral duty. Further reforms in voter registration may bring small increases in voter turnout, but a significant increase would require a fundamental change in the character of Americans.

The United States is proud to be the land of the free and the home of the brave. But when it comes to getting its citizens to vote on Election Day, the nation ranks with the world's laggards. Among Western industrialized nations, only tiny Switzerland has lower voter turnouts than ours.

This has been a long-standing problem in this country, yet historians and social scientists were rarely concerned with it before World War II. Voter turnout suffered a big drop in the 1920s and fluctuated after the New Deal realignment of the 1930s, when many people switched parties. It reached a crest in 1960, when 62.8 percent of eligible voters went to the polls—yet even then, participation was much lower than it had been, on average, during the last half of the 19th century.

In the early 1960s, President John F. Kennedy appointed a commission, chaired by Richard Scammon, to investigate the phenomenon of nonvoting and to recommend ways to improve turnout. The commission, finding that Americans were much less likely to vote than most Europeans and Canadians, produced an excellent report which stressed that citizens in this country faced greater obstacles to voting.

The report noted that the United States required its potential electorate to make two decisions: first to register to vote, often a considerable time before the election cycle, and then, only if registered, to vote on Election Day. Most other countries have a less cumbersome process. In Canada and Britain, state employees go house to house, much like census takers, registering people to vote. Hence, citizens are relieved of taking the initiative to register; their decision to cast a ballot is made on Election Day, reflecting how they feel at the end of campaigns after exposure to all that heat and glitter.

In addition, the American electoral system has emphasized length of residence in localities. Some states have required at least one year's residence in the same area; others, a stay of some months. Most countries with higher voting rates than ours do not have lengthy residency requirements. Also, some countries have permanent registration, as contrasted with the once predominant American practice of requiring registration before each election or of striking voters from the rolls if they failed to vote in one election.

The Scammon commission recommended that the conditions for voting be eased greatly. Kennedy agreed and recommended legislative changes to Congress and the states. Many of the reforms were enacted. Voter signups were made permanent in many states. Residential requirements were relaxed and the number of ways to register were increased. And yet, as Ruy A. Teixeira documents, the proportion of the electorate that voted dropped from more than three-fifths in 1968 to about one-half in the 1988 presidential contest. The numbers are much lower for state, congressional and local contests and for primaries, including those for the presidency. The overall figures went up slightly in 1992 when there were three major candidates for the White House, but the results of local elections in 1993 do not indicate this increase is holding.

---

*[Americans] lost confidence that changes brought about by elections would improve the situation much.*

---

These findings, of course, do not mean that the emphasis on structural impediments is wrong. Clearly more people will vote if it is easier to do so. What the continued falloff since the release of the Scammon commission report suggests is that some larger macrosocietal factors have been in play to reduce Americans' willingness to vote.

Looking at survey data, as Bill Schneider and I did in our book *The Confidence Gap*, one notices a large drop in the confidence that Americans have in institutions, particularly political ones. Beginning in the 1960s, Americans grew increasingly uneasy about the efficacy of their leaders. They lost confidence that changes brought about by elections would improve the situation much. With the exception of Ronald Reagan, each U.S. president turned out to be a disappointment to the electorate. Gridlock between Congress and the president and various scandals led to a disdain for all politicians, regardless of party. Consequently, voter turnout fell every year even though registration had become easier. The rejection of politics was reflected also in the decline of party identification, the growth of self-identified independents and the accompanying unwillingness to vote for candidates of the same party from election to election.

But declining voter turnout and the waning strength of traditional party affiliations are not limited to the U.S. Seemingly, voters in most stable democracies have lost faith in elections and their political leaders. Upstart parties and protest candidates such as Ross Perot have appeared in many countries, including Canada, France, Sweden, Italy, Belgium and Japan.

Even so, Americans continue to vote far less than other Western peoples. Close to three-fourths of Canadians, Britons, Scandinavians, Israelis and Japanese who are eligible to vote go to the polls on Election Day. Only the Swiss are in the the same range—around 50 percent—as we Americans. But the Swiss more or less maintain a permanent coalition of all parties, except for the Communists, so their elections are nearly meaningless.

## The American character and not voting

Why are we at the bottom of the electoral participation league? I would argue that it is for the same reason that we lead the Western world in crime and incarceration rates, as well as other indicators of deviant behavior. Americans are less inclined to conform or to obey the law than most Western peoples are. We are more individualistic and self-oriented and less communal and communitarian-minded. Ever since the founding of the republic, we have been more antistatist, distrustful and suspicious of government.

What has this to do with variations in voting behavior? This question may be answered by asking another question: Why should people vote? The civics textbooks tell us we should go to the polls to help elect officials who will represent our interests and give voice to our values. If conditions are bad, we should vote to help reverse policies; if corruption appears widespread, we should vote to help turn the rascals out.

Yet how realistic are such recommendations? As everyone knows, there is no chance that a single vote will determine the outcome of a presidential election or even gubernatorial or congressional contests. Hence, from a rational or self-interest point of view, voting involves effort for no gain. To go to a local office to register and then to go another day to vote may take hours—and prevent one from engaging in other rewarding activities. It seems, therefore, irrational to spend time on this ineffective task.

Ah, but even if there is no direct gain from voting, there is a moral reason for doing so, the political elite and the media tell us. As residents of a democratic country, we have the right to do what the citizens of dictatorships or corrupt polities cannot do. We should vote because it is what a good citizen of a democracy does. We can show the authoritarians what good democrats we are. Voting is a symbolic act by which we affirm our belief in freedom.

But compared with other Western peoples, Americans do not do what they should do or what they are told to do. The argument that we should be good citizens appeals to us less than it does to other democratic peoples. Consider the case of Canada. As I pointed out in *Continental Divide: The Values and Institutions of the United States and Canada*, Canadians not only have a much higher voting rate than Americans, they also have a lower incidence of crime. In addition, they exhibit more formal deference to the state and its laws. Statism, in the form of welfare activities, provision of services such as health care and government ownership of industry, is much more extensive in Canada than in the United States. Health care policy experts such as Alain Enthoven have argued that Canada's government-provider medical system would not work in this country because state medicine requires rationing of medical care—telling people to wait for surgery and other treatments. Americans would not put up with the need to wait the way Canadians do, they say.

Some time ago, on a visit to Ottawa to talk to a group of high-level civil servants, I had an experience that I related to my audience. I told them that as I had walked from my hotel to where I was to speak, I stopped at red lights. The Canadian officials began to laugh because they knew what was coming. At each stoplight, although there was no car in sight, people waited for the light to turn green before crossing the street. It is impossible to imagine comparable scenes in Washington, New York or other American cities.

---

*The argument that we should be good citizens appeals to us less than it does to other democratic peoples.*

---

Some years ago, Canada and the United States decided to drop their traditional but illogical systems of weights and measures—pounds, inches, miles, etc.—and adopt the metric system. Since they border each other, the two countries decided to implement the change at the same time, but they wanted to do it gradually. They announced that from a given date, metric would be the legal system, but that the old system still could be used for the next fifteen years. Well, if you have traveled in Canada, you know that when highway signs say the speed limit is 100, they mean kilometers per hour. The temperature is given in Celsius in Canada, not in Fahrenheit. When Canadians were told to go metric, they did; Americans did not.

In a similar vein, the two governments tried to change the dollar from a paper bill to a coin. Today, only the dollar coin is used north of the border; in the United States, the Susan B. Anthony dollar can be found only in Nevada and Atlantic City, New Jersey, where it is dropped into slot machines.

Voting is the same. Canadians are told that as good citizens they should vote, and 70 to 80 percent of them do, in both federal and provincial elections. But only one out of two Americans votes in presidential contests; many fewer, often around 20 to 25 percent, take part in the primaries to select presidential nominees.

The falloff in voting in the United States from the Kennedy era to the present, as well as the decline in participation in other nations, has occurred in tandem with the rise in crime and deviancy rates, such as illegitimacy and drug use. Nonvoting may be looked upon as a form of deviancy, whose increase is associated with comparable changes in other forms.

## Improving the situation

What can be done to improve the situation? The Scammon commission was on the right track. If we make the voting process easier, by allowing people to register when they obtain or renew drivers' licenses and/or by holding elections on Sundays as France and some other countries do, we would increase the proportion of those showing up at the polls, assuming nothing else happens, as in the sixties and early seventies, to affect the deviancy rates. But the ratio here will remain much lower than elsewhere, unless and until Americans become more law-abiding and more conformist.

Another change that could have a positive outcome is the addition of more political parties and candidates. More choices do have an effect, but again not a striking one. In any case, the one way to assure more diversity on the ballot is to change the electoral system and adopt proportional representation, in which a party's strength in a legislative body is determined by the total percentage of votes that it wins. But few Americans or U.S. leaders would favor such a dramatic change.

Hence, I conclude that we can tinker with the electoral system, make voting easier and raise the number of voters a bit. But, fundamentally, what makes a difference in voter turnout over time and among nations are macroscopic factors that influence the degree of conformism or deviance, or in extreme cases, severe crises, which mobilize voters to try to change the government.

But no one would like to see such events in order to change the ratio of voters to nonvoters.

Rather, I assume we would prefer to be like the happy Swiss, who maintain peace and prosperity and have reduced partisan conflict and electoral participation to what probably is about as low a level as possible in the modern world.

# 5

# Voting in America Is Limited to the Economic Elite

## John Kenneth Galbraith

*John Kenneth Galbraith is the Paul M. Warburg Professor of Economics emeritus at Harvard University and the author of* The Culture of Contentment, *from which this viewpoint is excerpted.*

Only the economically advantaged in America vote in elections. Because this economic class controls the nation's economy, both the Democratic and Republican parties limit their attention and efforts to political policies that will benefit the rich. The economically disadvantaged in America—who could become the majority of voters—do not vote because such political policies will not benefit them.

In the past, it is clear, the contented and the self-approving were a small minority in any national entity; left outside were the majority of the citizenry. Now in the United States the favored are numerous, greatly influential of voice and a majority of those who vote. This, and not the division of voters as between political parties, is what defines modern American political behavior. This, and not the much celebrated circumstance of charismatic political leaders and leadership, is what shapes modern politics. The leaders, a point sufficiently emphasized, are a reflection of their supporting constituency. Dominating and omnipresent on television, in the polls and in the press, they are passive or accommodating as to the political reality. Of that they are the product. Less dramatic but not dissimilar is the situation in other industrial countries, a matter on which there will be a later word.

## Parties and the politics of contentment

The Republican Party in the United States is the accepted representative of the comfortable and contented, the effective instrument of the economic principles and political behavior patterns identified therewith. There are, as always, a number of dissonant voices. Some formal dissent has long been heard from within the party as to macroeconomic policy, with budget deficits being specifically subject to grave verbal expressions of alarm. Overwhelmingly, however, the Republican Party accepts the commitment to short-run serenity as opposed to longer-run concern. It stands for a diminished role of government, exceptions for military expenditure, financial rescue and Social Security apart. Taxation is powerfully resisted; it is accepted that the rich and the relatively affluent need the incentive of good income as, if said more discreetly, the poor are deserving of their poverty. In presidential elections since 1980, the commitment of the Republicans to the policies of contentment has been the source of their marked success—victories by substantial majorities of those voting. Their Democratic opponents have found themselves faced with a seemingly intractable problem, and this they have generally resolved by also aligning themselves with the beliefs and the needs of the contented. Since the Republicans have a longer tradition of and a greater aptitude for satisfying this particular constituency, the Democrats have been defeated.

Many who vote Democratic, perhaps a majority, are, in fact, strongly committed to the politics of contentment. They are Democrats by local or family tradition. In the South and Southeast especially, but elsewhere as well, they combine inherited and regional attitudes with the economics of personal contentment and are openly known as *conservative* Democrats. They would vote Republican were there any threat of serious onslaught on the policies of contentment, and many have, in fact, made the transition. This they would all certainly do, were a Democratic presidential candidate to make a concerted political bid for those not similarly favored—those, as a prime example, who live in the desolation of the large inner cities. No action on behalf of the latter—improved welfare payments, more low-income housing, general health care, better schools, drug rehabilitation—could be taken without added public cost, and from this would come the decisive threat of higher taxation. Accordingly, in a dominant Democratic view, reference to such effort must be downplayed or, as necessary, avoided. It looms large in conversation, small in declared intent. Liberals, as they are known, are especially warned: whatever their personal opinion as to the larger well-being or the longer future, they must be practical. If they want to win, they must not invade the community of contentment. Some, and perhaps a considerable number, would feel obliged to desert a candidate strongly committed to the underclass and those now nonparticipant in the electoral system. The shock effect to comfort would even here be too severe.

## Money, the media, and the contented

There are, of course, other factors that support the politics of contentment. In the United States there is the powerful effect of money on public attitudes and political action, and money, in singular measure, is what the contented majority enjoys and deploys. It is to this audience that television and the press are directed. In consequence, the perception of government as an onerous and unnecessary burden, the presumptively self-inflicted wounds of the poor, even the cover stories emphasizing the high social utility of the returns to the rich, acquire acceptance as the reputable view. Inevitably, the commonly believed becomes the truth. Those who appeal too obviously to the poor are said to be not only politically impractical, they are in conflict with accepted reality. It helps, none can doubt, that those who report and comment on political matters—the representatives of the media—themselves belong to the contented majority, as do those who employ them or provide the income that sustains their employment. To be sure, the public and journalistic ethic requires that this never be admitted; there can, however, be surrender to a subdued but persuasive influence when the influence is unrecognized by those so surrendering.

And there is the more direct effect of money. This, indeed, is much discussed in our time. Elections have become exceedingly expensive, and, in one subtle or less subtle fashion or another, public salaries are supplemented from private sources. The sources of the needed funds are all but invariably the economically comfortable. They must be accorded deference, for it is from them that comes the wherewithal to contest elections as well as, in the frequent case, to sustain an agreeable personal living standard.

The political strategy, as rather loosely it is called, of Democratic candidates in recent presidential elections follows from the controlling factors just mentioned. There emerges here the self-styled political expert, even genius, who, being relentlessly available, is celebrated by the unduly susceptible representatives of the media. The amply advertised qualification for such a job is normally some past success in a secondary electoral contest, there being a still unrevealed certainty that he, or somewhat exceptionally she, will now lose the next one. In fact, the principal talent necessary is an accomplished mastery of elementary arithmetic.

From this modest mathematical competence comes the conclusion: to win, one must subtract voters from the other side. Accordingly, a Democratic presidential candidate must be no less acquiescent to the contented majority than the Republican. This requires that he make no serious bow to the nonparticipating, nonvoting minority; that would arrest all recruitment from the opposition with the further chance of losing comfortable Democratic voters.[1] In consequence of the foregoing, all recent presidential elections have been fought between twin exponents of the broad position of the contented majority. In 1988 the Democratic candidate, Michael Dukakis, largely abandoning the issues that might be adverse to the culture of contentment, made as his principal claim his "competence." Not surprisingly, the traditional and seemingly more reliable exponent of comfort [George Bush] won. Many decades ago President Harry S. Truman observed in a memorable comment that when there was a choice between true conservatives and those in pragmatic approximation thereto, the voters would always opt for the real thing.

## Exceptions to the rule

While the foregoing is the broad rule by which American electoral politics should be understood, there are, as in the case of all political matters, exceptions to be noted.

There is, first, the intruding role of international relations, and notably that of armed conflict. The major wars of this century—the two World Wars, the Korean and the war in Vietnam—were fought under Democratic auspices. In all four cases, the immediate instinctive support was strong; with the exception of World War II, the ultimate effect, however, was to bring the political opposition back into office. The public preference, even that of the more ardent supporters of military expenditure, is for short, comfortable, successful and not unduly expensive wars. These the Republicans have provided in Grenada [1983], Panama [1989–90] and Iraq [1991]. The Democratic fate has been wars of enduring pain, high fiscal cost and, in the case of Korea and Vietnam, with no dramatically successful conclusion.

> *Now in the United States the favored are numerous, greatly influential of voice and a majority of those who vote.*

There is also the somewhat different circumstance that applies to candidates for state and local office and particularly for the Congress. Here for traditional reasons, and largely in the South, it is possible for Democrats to appeal to the comfortable and contented and win election. In the larger cities and in older industrial areas, on the other hand, the Democrats must appeal to the socially concerned and to the discontented or dissatisfied, which in the particular constituency make up an electoral majority. The combination of these three sources of support—the traditional, the socially concerned and the discontented—has enabled the Democrats to maintain a majority in the two houses of Congress, but it has been at the cost of a sharp split between the traditionalists who serve the politics of contentment and those who have constituencies of comparative discontent or who are otherwise susceptible thereto.

## Why the discontented do not vote

Two matters concerning the politics of contentment remain. Those responding to its persuasion are a majority of those voting in the United States; they are not, as we have sufficiently seen, a majority of the adult population. Some who do not vote are illegal aliens; more are recently arrived from less favored lands and are awaiting citizenship. Thus, for some members of the underclass, squalor and privation are not exceptional, and there may be a sense of gratitude from having escaped something worse. However, the larger justification for not voting is that, for the reasons just given, it is an idle exercise for the eligible poverty-ridden citizen. It is rightly perceived that the difference between the two parties on the immediately affecting issues is inconsequential; accordingly, why bother to decide between them? Thus the majority rule of the contented is or has been ensured.

It follows further that presidential and legislative action or, more seriously, inaction, however adverse and alienating the effect on the socially excluded—homelessness, hunger, inadequate education, drug affliction, poverty in general—is under the broad sanction of democracy. A disturbing parallel emerges here. Prior to the great revolt of 1989–90 in Eastern Europe, dissatisfaction and alienation were under the broad gloss of socialism; if the people had socialism, they could not be unhappy. The case is now similar in language in the United States: this is the democratic system; systemically it is above error. The fact that a full half of the population does not participate in presidential elections, yet fewer in congressional contests, does not go unnoticed, but it also does not impair the assumption that democracy is controlling and benign.

Finally, there is the question of whether, and to what extent, the politics of contentment, which is so evident in the United States, extends to other industrial countries. There can be little doubt that it does. In the United Kingdom a contented majority ensured the rule of the government of Margaret Thatcher for eleven years, even though in the Midlands and to the north unemployment and exclusion were a continuing source of social discontent.

Unlike the Democrats in the United States, however, the British Labour Party, its more extreme and vocal dissidents kept largely under control, has continued to be seen as an alternative to the contented majority. In consequence, its members have still considered elections a worthwhile opportunity, and they have still gone to the polls to vote. They have also gained strength as the more dramatic actions of Mrs. Thatcher's government, most notably the poll tax as a substitute for local property levies (since partly repealed), have discountenanced the less affluent of the contented majority. In consequence, the political position of contentment may now be rather less secure in Britain than in the United States. And perhaps the case is the same in Canada, where a conservative government has by taxation and trade policy[2] somewhat similarly narrowed the political base of contentment.

---

*Those who appeal too obviously to the poor are said to be not only politically impractical, they are in conflict with accepted reality.*

---

In Western Europe there has been a different development. There, in Scandinavia, Germany, the Low Countries, Austria, France and Switzerland, strong social legislation has brought most of the citizenry into the contented majority. And accompanying and supporting this development has been the already mentioned large importation of labor from lower-wage countries to replace those of the contented who have removed themselves from hard, nonprestigious physical toil. With some noteworthy exceptions, these foreign workers do not or cannot vote, but since they are there as an exercise of their own will, they do not complain about being disenfranchised or they are not able to do so. Accordingly, the position of the contented majority in Western Europe, under whatever political label, seems relatively secure.

A final word on politics. As in economics nothing is certain save the certainty that there will be firm prediction by those who do not know. It is possible that in some election, near or far, a presidential candidate will emerge in the United States determined to draw into the campaign those not now impelled to vote. Conceivably those so attracted—those who are not threatened by higher taxes and who are encouraged by the vision of a new governing community committed to the rescue of the cities and the impacted underclass—could outnumber those lost because of the resulting invasion of contentment. If this happens, the effort would succeed.

It will be evident from these pages that that is not a glowing prospect.

## Notes

1. Having been a frequent speechwriter in presidential elections beginning with the Roosevelt campaign in 1940, I have had a close exposure to the above-mentioned arithmetical basis of political strategy and to its use by the current political strategist. As I've often told, he has leaned over my shoulder on the candidate's airplane to watch the words of a speech in progress on my typewriter.

   "Professor, you can't say that."

   "It's what our man believes, what the people need."

   "Look, if you say that, you will alienate those who are already most against us."

2. Specifically, the free trade agreement with the United States, which has resulted in Canada's loss in plants, employment and customers to its southern neighbor.

# 6

# Americans Vote Based on Religious and Cultural Ties

Lyman A. Kellstedt, John C. Green,
James L. Guth, and Corwin E. Smidt

*Lyman A. Kellstedt is a professor of political science at Wheaton College in Wheaton, Illinois. John C. Green is a professor of political science at the University of Akron, Ohio. James L. Guth is a professor of political science at Furman University in Greenville, South Carolina. Corwin E. Smidt is a professor of political science at Calvin College in Grand Rapids, Michigan.*

Many political scientists hold the conventional view that economic conditions are the primary influence on voter behavior. But religious and cultural affiliations form the basis of long-term voting coalitions, while economic status and economic conditions have only a short-term effect on voting. An analysis of the 1992 election shows that George Bush was defeated not primarily because the economy was in bad shape, but because traditionally Republican cultural coalitions did not support him. Future electoral coalitions will likely form along the lines of more-religious Americans versus less-religious Americans.

What really happened in the 1992 presidential election? And what does it tell us about American politics at the turn of the century? Although postmortems are always a tricky business, interpreting the 1992 election is particularly so. The defeat of an incumbent President, the election of the first "baby boomer" by a slim plurality, and the extraordinary campaign of an independent candidate are only the more obvious reasons for the special attention that 1992 is likely to be paid in the history books. But the question is, how will historians understand this election? They will certainly fail to do so adequately unless they offer proper recognition to the crucial influence of religious and cultural factors.

Most accounts of the 1992 election hinge on the economy. Bush lost, it is said, because the economy was sick and Republicans did not offer a plausible cure. As the sign in Clinton's campaign headquarters read: "It's

Lyman A. Kellstedt, John C. Green, James L. Guth, and Corwin E. Smidt, "It's the Culture, Stupid! 1992 and Our Political Future," *First Things*, April 1994. Reprinted with permission.

the economy, stupid!" This interpretation of the election fits nicely with the conventional view of American politics, held by academics and journalists alike, that party coalitions and electoral outcomes are rooted in economic self-interest. Thus, the combination of voters' economic status, the performance of the economy—and governmental policies affecting both—serves as the primary motivation for the vote. From this perspective, disputes over abortion, gay rights, and other so-called social issues are, at most, temporary diversions from normal economic preoccupations. Some observers have even reinterpreted social issue and foreign policy controversies as expressions of economic distress, arguing, in effect, that the only real values in politics are material ones.

## Culture, not economics, determines voting patterns

This conventional wisdom is not so much wrong as wrongly stated. While economic conditions clearly influence the vote, and often dramatically, the effects of such conditions are channeled through the cultural bedrock of the American party system. Most pundits and scholars do not realize that the basic "building blocs" of American party coalitions have always been cultural groups, whether in 1852, 1892, 1932, or 1992. And religious traditions, comprised of denominations and churches with shared values and worldviews, have always been among the most important of these. Year in and year out, the reaction to parties, candidates, and issues on the part of Evangelical, Mainline, and Black Protestants, Catholics, Jews, and Seculars is critical to understanding elections. The conventional wisdom, then, has it backwards: cultural affinities constitute the long-term basis of electoral alignments, introducing fundamental values into politics and structuring the debate over them, while economic forces generate temporary disruptions of these culturally defined alignments.

Thus while economic distress was critical to the electoral outcome in 1992, its effects are best understood within the cultural context of the vote. Religious traditions tied most closely to the Republican Party were less swayed by economic considerations than were their Democratic counterparts, and the least religiously observant voters in both traditions were the ones most influenced by economic woes. But of even greater significance, the conventional economic interpretation masks vital shifts in the cultural basis of party coalitions that were clearly visible in the election returns.

> *Cultural affinities constitute the long-term basis of electoral alignments, introducing fundamental values into politics and structuring the debate over them.*

Simply put, the historic conflict between rival coalitions of religious traditions is being replaced by a new division between more-religious and less-religious people across traditions. This emerging alignment opens new fault lines in the cultural bedrock of party coalitions and rechannels the effects of short-term economic conditions as well. The beginnings of this new alignment were recognized in Robert Wuthnow's discovery of the "restructuring of American religion," in Richard John Neuhaus' complaint about the "naked public square," and in James Davison Hunter's warnings of "culture wars." These divisions appeared first among elites but are now poised to play a major role among the citizenry at large.

## Economic concerns within cultural alignments

The notion that economics is the foundation of American partisan alignments has a rich pedigree, reaching back to the Federalist Papers, forward through Karl Marx and his followers, to modern, positivist social science. What is often forgotten is that assertions of economic primacy in public life often were—and still are—part of a distinctive political agenda. Consensus-oriented political leaders, advocates of economic modernization, and professional social scientists have all argued, in one way or another, that economic self-interest does—and should—matter most in politics. Political elites typically want to avoid the animosity associated with religious and cultural disputes, business leaders seek to promote the growth and stability of a modern industrial economy, and social scientists hope to construct objective, "value-free" theories of society. Although these goals may well be meritorious, the almost credal commitment to the primacy of economics has been intellectually costly, obscuring key elements of American politics.

Other perspectives have been available: a veritable host of historians—Paul Kleppner, Robert Swierenga, Richard Jensen, and Ronald Formisano, to name only a few—have demonstrated that American political parties have always been coalitions of "ethnocultural" or "ethnoreligious" groups rather than economic or class-based alliances. The Whigs, and later the Republicans, were the party of the culturally dominant Protestant churches. This coalition represented the cultural "haves" who sought to define the norms for the rest of the nation. In opposition, the Democrats represented the cultural "have-nots," minority religions like Catholics, Jews, "free thinkers," and some sectarian Protestants, such as Southern Baptists, who shared an interest in resisting majority impositions. And not surprisingly, individuals most committed to their churches and denominations participated most fully in these alliances. Of course, cultural and economic inequalities were often related, but because of the limited scope of both government and the economy, cultural differences usually prevailed. Although the exact composition of these partisan alliances varied by era, geography, and the salience of issues, the basic division between coalitions of competing religious traditions is still visible today.

These cultural alliances were necessitated by basic features of the American constitutional system. The First Amendment's establishment and free exercise provisions guaranteed two things: that there would be no state-sanctioned religion, and that there would be an extraordinary variety of churches, denominations, and cultural groups. But this same system also established single-member districts to elect the Congress and an Electoral College to choose the President, both of which fostered the familiar "two party system." The conjunction of the parties' goal to maximize votes and the desire of religious communities to voice their values made the aggregating of diverse groups into opposing coalitions both necessary and effective. Indeed, disputes between (and sometimes within) these cultural combines structured and restructured political debate, clothing the public square with a richly woven tapestry of values. Thus, American party politics has always involved "cultural wars," and the genius of our system has been its ability to contain these conflicts within civil and even productive bounds.

For most contemporary political scientists, however, the cultural basis for party coalitions, if recognized at all, ended with the New Deal, the historical backdrop for interpretations of contemporary politics. According to conventional wisdom, the New Deal era saw the elevation of economic issues to the center of the public agenda: the failures of laissez-faire economic policies were redressed by national programs intended to redistribute income, creating in their wake a powerful new class-based alignment that pitted the economic "have-nots" against the "haves."

Although not without considerable validity, this interpretation is much enriched by adding to the picture the profound cultural forces behind the New Deal. Long before the 1929 stock market crash, the dominant WASP (white Anglo-Saxon Protestant) social and political ethos was under intense pressure from rival cultures with roots in European Catholic and Jewish immigration and concentrated in burgeoning metropolitan areas. In many respects, the New Deal was less about income redistribution than about the recognition of "group rights" benefitting these cultural challengers, a recognition embedded in such policies as the fostering of labor unions, public works programs, and social insurance. Even the makeup of the resulting New Deal electoral coalition is most easily described in religious and cultural terms: an alliance of Catholic and Jewish ethnics, with help from Southern and Black Protestants, and a leavening of urban cosmopolitans.

> *It is cultural alignments that provide the foundation of electoral politics, setting the context for the impact of more immediate economic concerns.*

The key point is this: in order to have political relevance, economic conditions must be *interpreted*. Religion and culture supply a powerful framework for such interpretation, providing both the larger worldview and the more specific values by which voters may understand the contemporary world. Since religion and culture are deeply embedded in the way people are raised and in the communities in which they live, this framework remains quite stable, changing only gradually even in the fast-paced modern world. But by the same token, the nationalization—and globalization—of markets means that changes in economic conditions nowadays affect all religious and cultural groups simultaneously. Thus it is cultural alignments that provide the foundation of electoral politics, setting the context for the impact of more immediate economic concerns.

Unfortunately, most political scientists and many survey researchers have missed this pattern, either because they tend to ignore history or because they do not understand religion. As a result, little intellectual capital has been invested in the arduous task of understanding America's bewildering array of religious and cultural groups. This neglect has been particularly costly for understanding the variegated electoral faces of Protestantism: even today, most polls use the term "Protestant" as if it were a meaningful category.

Gradually, however, the realities of cultural politics are becoming evident even to secular academics, and some political scientists have developed survey items that distinguish among religious traditions as well as levels of religious commitment (the latter measured by church attendance, devotional practices, and the like).

To oversimplify a complex picture, these new approaches reveal three politically relevant groups among Protestants: the Mainline, Evangelical, and Black Protestant traditions. Combined with more accurate identification of Catholics, Jews, and Seculars (or religiously uncommitted), as well as other smaller traditions, these categories allow analysts to identify both the continuity of historic religious coalitions and the transformations currently underway. The picture is enhanced even more by taking into account levels of religious commitment. In the past, the religiously committed in each tradition were at the forefront of the rival coalitions. In an important contemporary transformation, coalitions increasingly pit the religiously committed within each tradition against those with little or no commitment.

## Religious affiliations: the building blocs of parties

Despite the importance of economic conditions in 1992, then, religious and cultural alignments were very much in evidence in voting patterns. These alignments, in turn, are best understood in terms of a major cultural shift underway for more than a generation, but by no means complete. Since the New Deal a series of slow, but steady, changes has brought the cultural hegemony of Mainline Protestantism to an end, and with it the predominant set of values associated with the old term, "Protestant." These cultural changes are too familiar to require elaboration here: rapid upward mobility, the expansion of higher education, the growth and development of the mass media, the end of legal segregation, and alterations in women's roles. We can illustrate the political implications of this cultural shift by examining the transitions in voting patterns of the major religious traditions between 1960 and 1992.

Mainline Protestants were traditionally the backbone of the Republican coalition. Their large numbers (approximately two-fifths of the population in 1960), their relatively high levels of religious commitment and political activity, and their conservative opinions on most issues all combined to produce formidable support for the GOP up and down the ticket. In the 1960 presidential election, for example, 69 percent of Mainliners voted Republican. By 1992, however, the situation had changed dramatically. Sharp declines in relative numbers (to about one-fifth of the population), even sharper reduction in religious commitment, and deep divisions on social issues sapped the Mainline's political strength and undermined its dominant position in the Republican Party. George Bush received only 39 percent of Mainline votes in the three-way race (or 50 percent of the two-party vote). Only their customarily high turnout and overrepresentation among GOP elites kept Mainliners from becoming distinctly junior partners in the Republican coalition. Interestingly enough, social issues such as abortion and gay rights were not central to Mainline defections from Bush in 1992. Rather, most defectors exhibited low levels of religious commitment and were dramatically influenced by short-term economic factors. Even so, few Mainline voters defected to Clinton, preferring the more culturally congenial Ross Perot.

If, over the past twenty years, the GOP had to rely primarily on Mainline Protestants, the party would have suffered electoral disasters far greater than that in 1992. But the Republicans benefitted greatly from changes within another religious tradition, as Evangelical Protestants simultaneously moved away from Democratic partisanship and toward both greater political involvement and Republican partisanship. Beginning with their reaction to the Catholic John F. Kennedy's presence on the Democratic ticket in 1960 (when 60 percent voted Republican), Evangelicals steadily moved away from preference for Democratic candidates, a movement interrupted only temporarily by the candidacies of Southerners Lyndon Johnson and Jimmy Carter, the latter a fellow Evangelical. By 1992, Evangelicals were George Bush's best supporters, giving him 56 percent of their votes in the three-way race (and 67 percent of the two-party vote); and to a greater extent than ever before they backed Republican candidates all the way down the ticket. This shift was amplified by the Evangelicals' steady religious market share since 1960 (about one-quarter of the population) and consistent conservatism on social and foreign policy issues—a conservatism that gave evidence of expanding to include traditional Republican economic issues. And their voting turnout increased somewhat since 1960, although still lagging a bit behind their Mainline cousins in 1992.

---

*Contemporary social issue disputes, such as that over abortion, are not temporary aberrations, but rather the stuff of future politics.*

---

Thus a combination of factors has united white Protestants in the same coalition, with the former senior partner becoming a junior one in terms of total vote support for the GOP. Like all such coalitions, this new alignment is fraught with internal tensions, particularly over social issues. How these tensions will be resolved is a matter of conjecture, but in 1992 the new partners and their social issue conservatism helped George Bush far more than they hurt him. Not only did religious conservatives provide Bush with a lion's share of his votes, but they also expressed more positive views of the economy, largely interpreting the recession through the lens of their cultural allegiance. Given this situation, it is not surprising that few Evangelicals voted for Perot, and that those few who did showed lower levels of religious commitment.

In 1960, the Kennedy campaign achieved a record Democratic vote (82 percent) from Roman Catholics. The large size of this constituency (one-fifth of the adult population), their high levels of religious commitment and turnout, and strongly liberal opinions on the issues of the day all combined to make Catholics a formidable Democratic voting bloc. Between 1960 and 1992, Catholics increased in relative numbers (to almost one-quarter of the population), but experienced a decline in religious commitment that paralleled the Protestant Mainline. Following which, as in the Mainline, serious rifts opened among Catholics on social and economic issues. The result was increased Catholic defection to the GOP, but by two very different groups: traditionalists motivated by social and foreign policy issues, and the less religiously observant enticed by Reagan's promises of prosperity. In 1992, many of the fair-weather Catholic "economic Republicans" returned to the Democratic fold, giving Bill Clinton 45 percent of the Catholic vote in the three-way race (59 percent of the two-party vote). But just as religiously committed Evangelical and Mainline Protestants were much more likely to vote Republican than their nominally religious brethren, regularly attending white Catholics gave Bush a narrow plurality over Clinton (41 percent to 39 percent), while less-observant Catholics gave Clinton a bigger margin (44 percent to 33 percent). Again, as with the Protestants, Catholic Perot voters were drawn from the least religiously observant.

---

*A new cultural underpinning to party alignments emerged in 1992, pitting coalitions of more- and less-religious people against one another.*

---

The electoral contributions of two smaller religious traditions, Jews and Black Protestants, should be noted as well. Jews are both culturally and economically liberal, and have been solidly Democratic since long before 1960. As for the Black Protestants, prior to 1964 they included a significant Republican minority, but since then have been overwhelmingly Democratic. Both groups were crucial elements of Clinton's coalition in 1992; and although there are religious conservatives in both traditions, the GOP has made only marginal inroads among them so far.

Almost unnoticed has been the growth and political relevance of the Secular segment of the population. Given the sporadic attention given to religion by survey researchers, it has been difficult to track the expansion of this group with certainty. The best estimates suggest that Seculars constituted less than one-tenth of the population in 1960, but had expanded to at least one-fifth by 1992. Although many observers see this growth only as evidence of the increasing irrelevance of religion, the nonreligious represent an important cultural group, as liberal on social issues as the most committed religious people are conservative. Seculars tend to vote Democratic at all levels, with 54 percent supporting Kennedy in 1960, but there have been exceptions to this pattern; in 1980, 68 percent voted for Ronald Reagan on the basis of short-term economic considerations. In 1992, however, Seculars moved dramatically back into the Democratic column, with 55 percent supporting Clinton in a three-way race (73 percent of the two-party vote). While Seculars constitute a partial replacement for the departed Evangelicals in the Democratic coalition, their impact has been lessened by their low rates of turnout.

In sum, then, 1992 voting patterns reveal historic cultural alignments, albeit reshuffled by the cultural changes of the last generation, and modified by the short-term effects of a weak economy. Bush attracted a coalition of Evangelical and Mainline Protestants, joined by some strongly religious Catholics, while Clinton won with a coalition of less religiously adherent Catholics, most Blacks, Jews, and Seculars, and with a smattering of Protestants. Perot picked up the votes of the economically disaffected with low religious commitments.

These patterns show the limitations of defining electoral alignments largely in terms of short-term economic factors. Evangelical and high-commitment Mainline Protestants were generally less affluent and hence most affected by the recession, and yet they stood most firmly behind Bush. Meanwhile, Jewish and Secular voters were generally more affluent and least burdened by hard times, yet they were among the strongest supporters of Bill Clinton. Economic conditions had their largest effect among Perot's supporters, who were the most disconnected from social and political life—a fact reflected in their intense disgust with government and politics. Beyond demonstrating the power of culture in electoral alignments, however, 1992 reveals the effects of a generation of cultural polarization, and the emergence of a new kind of electoral alignment.

## A new alignment of religious affiliation

The new cultural politics in 1992 differs from past alignments in kind rather than degree. The historic conflict between coalitions of rival religious traditions is being replaced by a new division between more-religious and less-religious people across those traditions. Our analysis suggests that one of the emerging coalitions will be united by belief in God, an understanding that such belief has implications for public life, and a preference for religious language in political discourse. The opposite coalition will be united by nontheistic or at least nonorthodox beliefs, the policy implications of such beliefs, and hostility to religious language in political debate. If this analysis is correct, Evangelicals and committed members of other religious traditions could find themselves united in the Republican Party facing Seculars and less committed members in other traditions among the Democrats.

From this perspective, contemporary social issue disputes, such as that over abortion, are not temporary aberrations, but rather the stuff of future politics, where an agenda of "traditional values" confronts an agenda of "personal liberation" or what Ronald Inglehart has called, somewhat misleadingly, "postmaterial" values. Such disputes include a host of related issues, such as women's rights, birth control, sex education, gay rights, and regulation of pornography, and with only a little difficulty could be expanded to broader topics such as family policy, health insurance, public school curricula, employment practices, and funding for the arts. More important, such political agendas might eventually incorporate economic questions like taxes, business regulation, and free trade. Finally, voters tied firmly to either coalition would then interpret changing economic conditions in light of these prior, cultural, allegiances.

This kind of alignment is new to the United States, but divisions of this sort have been common in European democracies for centuries. While it is unclear how quickly such an alignment will solidify, it will introduce a new set of values into public life and restructure the debate about them, supplementing, if not replacing, older cultural alignments. If the resulting structure seems complex, we should remember Walter Dean Burnham's observation that each succeeding realignment of American voting habits leaves behind a residue never entirely absorbed into the "new" structure of political debate.

Indeed, one must resist the temptation to think of this emerging alignment in terms of the conventional liberal-conservative continuum. The "religious" coalition, for example, might break the mold on welfare policy by combining generosity with curbs on anti-social behavior, or the "secular" alliance could redefine a family policy to balance the concerns of adults with the needs of children. In fact, such departures from present thinking are quite likely because these new coalitions will require significant adjustments among participating religious traditions. For instance, more orthodox Evangelical and Mainline Protestants will have to learn to cooperate among themselves, as well as with traditionalist Catholics and Jews, and with other religious conservatives, such as Mormons. Likewise, less orthodox religionists and Seculars will need to develop a firm moral and ethical basis for their politics. Both sides will need to define themselves in positive terms rather than only in opposition to the real or imagined excesses of the other.

What the new alignment is sure to bring, however, is an end to the historic dominance of large, pluralistic denominations, such as the United Methodist and Roman Catholic churches, which have presumed to speak broadly for societal values. Once the linchpins of the traditional party coalitions, these bodies will increasingly come under pressure from both the religious right and the secular left. As a result, their ability to maintain a distinctive voice in public debate, let alone a consensual one, will be extremely difficult.

Which side of this new alignment will prevail? At this juncture it is unclear who are the cultural "haves" and who are the "have-nots." This situation can be illustrated by the new core constituencies of the GOP and the Democrats, Evangelicals and Seculars, respectively. Both groups like to claim that they are "disadvantaged" in the public square and victims of "cultural aggression," but neither is lacking in resources for offense or defense. The vast institutional empire of Evangelicals, ranging from thousands of local churches to publishing houses, colleges, and mass media outlets, is quite impressive. But Seculars are linked closely to the nation's educational, journalistic, and scientific establishments to an equally impressive extent. Will the negative consequences of secularization bring the religious alliance more recruits? Will the continued advance of modernity give the nonreligious coalition better weaponry? Or will an even division of power obtain? While any final judgment is premature, the strong connections of the religious alliance to the grass roots suggest that the religious coalition may have an advantage in the immediate future, but that secularizing forces may gain the upper hand in the longer run.

Some observers find the emergence of this new alignment troubling because it generates unfamiliar kinds of conflict, but in a democracy conflict is often a prelude to consensus. Although there is no guarantee that cultural disputes can be kept within reasonable bounds, suppressing disagreement will not maintain the peace. Some disagreements are resolvable only by agreements to disagree or acceptance of the provisional nature of victories and defeats. After all, unhappiness with social and political outcomes is not disastrous if the losing positions were based on principle and if the political system provided a fair hearing for all sides. The view that good politics requires a detailed, preexisting consensus on values is as unwarranted as the notion that economics alone drives politics. In fact, the present restructuring of electoral alignments is a potent means of bringing neglected values to the fore and organizing the debate about them.

A cultural perspective on the 1992 election, then, suggests three conclusions. First, the conventional wisdom on the role of economic factors in elections is overstated; even in a year when such short-term factors were particularly strong, they operated within the context of long-term cultural alignments. Second, the basic building blocs of party coalitions are cultural groups, chief among them religious traditions, and continuity and change among these blocs is of lasting importance. Finally, a new cultural underpinning to party alignments emerged in 1992, pitting coalitions of more- and less-religious people against one another.

These conclusions suggest that the "public square" has never been— and can never be—denuded of values, despite the best efforts of some groups to promote the historically false argument that American society is based on a strict separation of faith and public life. The answer to the "naked public square," George Weigel reminds us, is to reconstruct civil society on the basis of common values. Cultural disputes have always been—and always will be—integral parts of American elections, but, as Stephen Carter argues, an enhanced appreciation of religion is an effective antidote to cultural "warfare." In any case, it is clear that contemporary observers and future historians alike ignore religious and cultural factors at their peril.

# 7

# The Dominant Parties No Longer Represent the Voters' Interests

## E.J. Dionne Jr.

*E.J. Dionne Jr. is a columnist for the* Washington Post *and author of* Why Americans Hate Politics, *from which this viewpoint is excerpted.*

Americans have become discontented with politics. The main reason for their dissatisfaction is that liberal and conservative politicians continue to fight the cultural civil wars of the 1960s over social issues such as race relations and feminism, while most voters would like to move on to new issues. Both major political parties—Democrat and Republican—use negative campaigns to try to strip support from their opponents rather than using positive campaigns to attract voters. This negativity and the polarization between the parties over old social issues increase voters' disaffection.

On the weekend before January 16, 1991, Americans watched an extraordinary event: The Congress of the United States, with seriousness, conviction, and moments of eloquence, debated one of the most serious issues imaginable—Should our country go to war?

After years of political game-playing, sound-bite mongering, and just plain foolishness, America's politicians demonstrated that they were, indeed, capable of coming to grips with each other's arguments. It was possible in American politics to debate an issue without questioning the motives of an adversary. It was possible to argue fiercely without leaving the country hopelessly divided. It was even possible to agree on a fundamental issue—in this case, the need to reverse Saddam Hussein's aggression against Kuwait—and then debate thoughtfully over the best means to reach the shared end.

There should, of course, be nothing remarkable about this. Democratic politics is supposed to be deliberative. It is supposed to be about people reasoning together. It is supposed to be about honest disagreement and civil argument.

Yet the event was remarkable because for so many years our politics has been trivial and even stupid. Americans have come to hate politics. We thus face the disturbing question: Does it take a war to make us take politics seriously?

## Americans are bored with politics

Over the last three decades, the faith of the American people in their democratic institutions has declined, and Americans have begun to doubt their ability to improve the world through politics. At a time when the people of Poland, Hungary, and Czechoslovakia are experiencing the excitement of self-government, Americans view politics with boredom and detachment. For most of us, politics is increasingly abstract, a spectator sport barely worth watching. Election campaigns generate less excitement than ever and are dominated by television commercials, direct mail, polling, and other approaches that treat individual voters not as citizens deciding their nation's fate, but as mere collections of impulses to be stroked and soothed.

True, we still praise democracy incessantly and recommend democracy to the world. But at home, we do little to promote the virtues that self-government requires or encourage citizens to believe that public engagement is worth the time. Our system has become one long-running advertisement against self-government. For many years, we have been running down the public sector and public life. Voters doubt that elections give them any real control over what the government does, and half of them don't bother to cast ballots.

Because of our flight from public life, our common citizenship no longer fosters a sense of community or common purpose. Social gaps, notably the divide between blacks and whites, grow wider. The very language and music heard in the inner city are increasingly estranged from the words and melodies of the affluent suburbs. We have less and less to do with each other, meaning that we feel few obligations to each other and are less and less inclined to vindicate each other's rights. The Persian Gulf War has raised disturbing questions about how we share the most basic burden of democratic citizenship: the obligation to defend the country in time of peril. Many black Americans felt that they were bearing a much larger share of this obligation than the rest of the nation. This was one cause for the finding of the public opinion polls that African Americans were far less likely than other Americans to support the war effort. Thus did our nation's racial divisions threaten to affect questions of national security.

*Americans have come to hate politics.*

The abandonment of public life has created a political void that is filled increasingly by the politics of attack and by issues that seem unimportant or contrived. In 1988, George Bush made the pollution of Boston Harbor and the furloughing of a convicted murderer central issues in his campaign for the presidency. Neither Boston Harbor nor prison furloughs mattered once Bush took office. The issues that will matter most in the nineties—the dangers in the Middle East, the changing face of the Soviet Union and Central Europe, the crisis in the banking system—were hardly discussed at all in 1988.

We are even uncertain about the meaning of America's triumph in the Cold War. We worry that the end of the Cold War will mean a diminished role for the United States in world history. Economic power is passing not only to Japan but also to a new Europe that is finally recovering from the self-inflicted wounds of two world wars.

The categories that have dominated our thinking for so long are utterly irrelevant to the new world we face. The international alliance assembled against Iraq would have been inconceivable just two years earlier. Indeed, the very weapons we used against Saddam's forces were built for a different conflict in a different place against a different enemy. So much of the debate over Iraq was shaped by the Vietnam conflict, as if the use of American force always means the same thing in every part of the world and against every adversary.

## The cultural war between liberalism and conservatism

Most of the problems of our political life can be traced to the failure of the dominant ideologies of American politics, liberalism and conservatism. The central argument of this viewpoint is that liberalism and conservatism are framing political issues as a series of false choices. Wracked by contradiction and responsive mainly to the needs of their various constituencies, liberalism and conservatism *prevent* the nation from settling the questions that most trouble it. On issue after issue, there is consensus on where the country should move or at least on what we should be arguing about; liberalism and conservatism make it impossible for that consensus to express itself.

To blame our problems on the failure of "ideologies" would seem a convenient way to avoid attaching responsibility to individuals. But to hold ideologies responsible for our troubles is, in fact, to place a burden on those who live by them and formulate them. It is also a way of saying that ideas matter, and that ideas, badly formulated, interpreted and used, can lead us astray. We are suffering from a false polarization in our politics, in which liberals and conservatives keep arguing about the same things when the country wants to move on.

The cause of this false polarization is the cultural civil war that broke out in the 1960s. Just as the Civil War dominated American political life for decades after it ended, so is the cultural civil war of the 1960s, with all its tensions and contradictions, shaping our politics today. We are still trapped in the 1960s.

The country still faces three major sets of questions left over from the old cultural battles: civil rights and the full integration of blacks into the country's political and economic life; the revolution in values involving feminism and changed attitudes toward child-rearing and sexuality; and the ongoing debate over the meaning of the Vietnam War, which is less a fight over whether it was right to do battle in that Southeast Asian country than an argument over how Americans see their nation, its leaders, and its role in the world.

It is easy to understand why conservatives would like the cultural civil war to continue. It was the *kulturkampf* [cultural struggle] of the 1960s that made them so powerful in our political life. Conservatives were able to destroy the dominant New Deal coalition by using cultural and social issues—race, the family, "permissiveness," crime—to split New Deal constituencies. The cultural issues, especially race, allowed the conservatives who took control of the Republican Party to win over what had been the most loyally Democratic group in the nation, white Southerners, and to peel off millions of votes among industrial workers and other whites of modest incomes.

The new conservative majority that has dominated presidential politics since 1968 is inherently unstable, since it unites upper-income groups, whose main interest is in smaller government and lower taxes, and middle- to lower-income groups, who are culturally conservative but still support most of the New Deal and a lot of the Great Society. The lower-income wing of the conservative coalition has tended to vote Republican for president, to express its cultural values, but Democratic for Congress, to protect its economic interests. Conservative politicians are uneasy about settling the cultural civil war because they fear that doing so would push their newfound supporters among the less well-to-do back toward the Democrats in presidential contests.

The broad political interests of liberals lie in settling the cultural civil war, but many liberals have an interest in seeing it continue. The politics of the 1960s shifted the balance of power within the liberal coalition away from working-class and lower-middle-class voters, whose main concerns were economic, and toward upper-middle-class reformers mainly interested in cultural issues and foreign policy. Increasingly, liberalism is defined not by its support for energetic government intervention in the economy but by its openness to cultural change and its opposition to American intervention abroad. The rise of the cultural issues made the upper-middle-class reformers the dominant voices within American liberalism. The reformers, no less than the conservatives, have a continuing interest in seeing the cultural civil war continue.

## Liberals and conservatives are stuck in the sixties

Indeed, what is striking about political events of the 1960s is that they allowed both of the nation's dominant ideologies, and both parties, to become vehicles for upper-middle-class interests. Both the 1964 Barry Goldwater campaign and the antiwar forces associated with George McGovern's 1972 candidacy were movements of the upper middle class imbued with a moral (or, in the eyes of their critics, moralistic) vision. These constituencies were *not* primarily concerned with the political issues that matter to less well-to-do voters—notably the performance of the nation's economy, the distribution of economic benefits, and the efficacy of the most basic institutions of government, including schools, roads, and the criminal justice system. While upper-middle-class reformers, left and right, argued about morality, anticommunism, imperialism, and abstract rights, a large chunk of the electorate was confined to the sidelines, wondering why the nation's political discussion had become so distant from their concerns.

By continuing to live in the 1960s, conservatives and liberals have distorted their own doctrines and refused to face up to the contradictions within their creeds. Both sides constantly invoke individual "rights" and then criticize each other for evading issues involving individual and collective responsibility. Each side claims to have a communitarian vision but backs away from community whenever its demands come into conflict with one of its cherished doctrines.

Conservatives claim to be the true communitarians because of their support for the values of "family, work, and neighborhood." Unlike liberals, conservatives are willing to assert that "community norms" should prevail on such matters as sex, pornography, and the education of children. Yet the typical conservative is unwilling to defend the interests of traditional community whenever its needs come into conflict with those of the free market. If shutting down a plant throws thousands in a particular community out of work, conservatives usually defend this assault on "family, work, and neighborhood" in the name of efficiency. Many of the things conservatives bemoan about modern society—a preference for short-term gratification over long-term commitment, the love of things instead of values, a flight from responsibility toward selfishness—result at least in part from the workings of the very economic system that conservatives feel so bound to defend. For conservatives, it is much easier to ignore this dilemma and blame "permissiveness" on "big government" or "the liberals."

> *We are suffering from a false polarization in our politics, in which liberals and conservatives keep arguing about the same things when the country wants to move on.*

The liberals often make that easy. Liberals tout themselves as the real defenders of community. They speak constantly about having us share each other's burdens. Yet when the talk moves from economic issues to culture or personal morality, liberals fall strangely mute. Liberals are uncomfortable with the idea that a virtuous community depends on virtuous individuals. Liberals defend the welfare state but are uneasy when asked what moral values the welfare state should promote—as if billions of federal dollars can be spent in a "value-free" way. Liberals rightly defend the interests of children who are born into poverty through no choice of their own. Yet when conservatives suggest that society has a vital interest in how the parents of these poor children behave, many liberals accuse the conservatives of "blaming the victim." When conservatives suggest that changing teenage attitudes toward premarital sex might reduce teen pregnancy, many liberals end the conversation by accusing the conservatives of being "prudes" or "out of touch."

Not all conservatives and liberals fall into the neat categories I have just described, and the questions each side raises about the other's proposals are often legitimate. It often *is* more efficient and socially beneficial to shut down a loss-making plant. It *is* unfair to condemn the poor for sexual practices that we celebrate when those engaging in them live in Hollywood or make millions of dollars in business.

Still, the way in which liberals and conservatives approach the problem of community is a good example of what I mean by false choices. In truth, America's cultural values are a rich and not necessarily contradictory mix of liberal instincts and conservative values. Polls (and our own intuitions) suggest that Americans believe in helping those who fall on hard times, in fostering equal opportunity and equal rights, in providing broad access to education, housing, health care, and child care. Polls (and our intuitions) also suggest that Americans believe that intact families do the best job at bringing up children, that hard work should be rewarded, that people who behave destructively toward others should be punished, that small institutions close to home tend to do better than big institutions run from far away, that private moral choices usually have social consequences. Put another way, Americans believe in social concern and self-reliance; they want to match rights and obligations; they think public moral standards should exist but are skeptical of too much meddling in the private affairs of others.

## False choices and polarized voters

One fair reaction to the above is to call it a catalogue of the obvious. But that is precisely the point: that the false choices posed by liberalism and conservatism make it extremely difficult for the perfectly obvious preferences of the American people to express themselves in our politics. We are encouraging an "either/or" politics based on ideological preconceptions rather than a "both/and" politics based on ideas that broadly unite us.

To be sure, free elections in a two-party system inevitably encourage polarization; voters who like some things about liberals or Democrats and some things about conservatives or Republicans end up having to choose one package or the other. In free elections, each side will always try to polarize the electorate in a way that will leave a majority standing on its side. But if free elections leave so many in the electorate dissatisfied with where they have to stand and push large numbers out of the electorate entirely, then it is fair to conclude that the political process is badly defective.

Moreover, after the election is over, parties have to govern. By putting such a premium on false choices and artificial polarization, our electoral process is making it harder and harder for electoral winners to produce what they were elected for: good government. The false polarization that may be inevitable at election time is carrying over into the policy debates that take place afterward. Political "positioning" may be necessary in an electoral campaign; when it becomes part of the intellectual debate, the talk becomes dishonest. Our intellectual life, which is supposed to clear matters up, produces only more false choices.

## Negative campaigns

In recent years, much has been written about the rise of "negative campaigning" and of the "killer" television spots that instantly bury a political candidate's chances. Much has also been said about the rise of the "character issue" and the seemingly incessant interest of the press in the private lives of politicians. A candidate's sex life or his draft record dominates the public discussion. What were once called "issues" are cast to one side. Taken together, these developments suggest that politics is destined to become ever more seamy. Democracy takes on all the dignity of mud wrestling. When American political consultants descended upon Eastern Europe to help "guide" newcomers to democracy in the ways of modern politics, there was much alarm. Why should newly founded democracies be "guided" toward the dismal stuff that we Americans call politics?

---

*What is striking about political events of the 1960s is that they allowed both of the nation's dominant ideologies, and both parties, to become vehicles for upper-middle-class interests.*

---

In explaining these sorry developments, we have tended, I believe, to focus too narrowly on the political *process* and not enough on the *content* of politics.

The focus on process is perfectly sensible as far as it goes. By allowing the paid, thirty-second television spot to become our dominant means of political communication, we have shaped our political life in certain directions. In a thirty-second spot, candidates and parties can only give impressions, appeal to feelings, arouse emotions. Wedged in the midst of ads for all manner of products, the political spot needs to grab its audience. This tends to rule out even thirty seconds of sober discussion of the issues. Sobriety rarely grabs anyone. Most democracies offer political parties and candidates significant blocks of time in which they can tell their stories. And most provide the time free. The fact that our spots must be paid for raises the cost of American campaigns far above the levels in most other democracies. Raising the cost of campaigns has heightened the importance of fund-raising. This forces politicians to spend an untoward amount of time raising money. It also gives lobbyists and political action committees undue influence on our politics and gives average voters much less. The strong and the wealthy tend to have the most money to give away.

Reformers have many good ideas on how the system can be improved. Allocating free or cheap television time to candidates and parties would help. Offering the time in blocks larger than thirty seconds would help, too. There is no shortage of ideas on how to reduce the influence of money on politics, including a variety of limitations on the size and kind of contributions that can be made and various schemes for total or partial public financing of campaigns. All these things would improve our politics.

But they would not, finally, cure our underlying political problems. The real problem is not the spots themselves but what is said in them. Why is it that they focus so insistently on either character assassination or divisive social issues that leave the electorate so angry and dissatisfied? This is not a technical question but a political issue. Once upon a time, most of the thirty-second spots that ran on television were *positive*. They sought to mobilize voters behind causes and candidates they could believe in, not in opposition to ideas and constituencies they loathed. The content of political advertising suggested that, on balance, politicians were more concerned with getting things done than with foiling the nasty designs of others.

At its best, democratic politics is about what Arthur Schlesinger, Jr., calls "the search for remedy." The purpose of democratic politics is to solve problems and resolve disputes. But since the 1960s, the key to winning elections has been to reopen the same divisive issues over and over again. The issues themselves are not reargued. No new light is shed. Rather, old resentments and angers are stirred up in an effort to get voters to cast yet one more ballot of angry protest. Political consultants have been truly ingenious in figuring out creative ways of tapping into popular anger about crime. Yet their spots do not solve the problem. Endless arguments about whether the death penalty is a good idea do not put more cops on the street, streamline the criminal justice system, or resolve some of the underlying causes of violence.

The decline of a "politics of remedy" creates a vicious cycle. Campaigns have become negative in large part because of a sharp decline in popular faith in government. To appeal to an increasingly alienated electorate, candidates and their political consultants have adopted a cynical stance which, they believe with good reason, plays into popular cynicism about politics and thus wins them votes. But cynical campaigns do not resolve issues. They do not lead to "remedies." Therefore, problems get worse, the electorate becomes *more* cynical—and so does the advertising.

## The decline of political coalitions

Politicians engage in symbolic rather than substantive politics for another reason: Liberals and conservatives alike are uncertain about what remedies they can offer without blowing their constituencies apart. The two broad coalitions in American political life—liberal and Democratic, conservative and Republican—have become so unstable that neither side can afford to risk very much. That is because the ties that bind Americans to each other, to their communities, and thus to their political parties have grown ever weaker.

The party system of the New Deal Era was relatively stable because definable groups voted together and largely held together, even in bad times. Now, almost everything conspires against group solidarity. Unions are in trouble—and conservatives have done everything they could to weaken them. The new jobs in the service industries promote individualism. The decline of the small town and the old urban ethnic enclaves and the rise of new suburbs, exurbs, and condominium developments further weaken social solidarity. Old urban neighborhoods feel abandoned by the liberal politicians whom they once counted on for support.

---

*Since the 1960s, the key to winning elections has been to reopen the same divisive issues over and over again.*

---

In the new politics, each voter is studied and appealed to as an *individual*. This is both the cause and effect of the rise of polling and television advertising. It also explains the increasing harshness of political attack and counterattack. In the old politics, voters felt real loyalties, which could be appealed to in a positive way. Political loyalties were reinforced by other forms of group solidarity. Now, insofar as voters identify with

groups, it is often with abstract national groups rather than concrete local ones. An Italian machinist in a Detroit suburb may identify himself
more with his fellow gun owners than with his ethnic group, his neighborhood, or his fellow workers. Since he believes that politics will do little to improve his life or that of his community, he votes defensively: If
the government won't do anything *for* him, he damn well won't let it do
anything *against* him, such as tax him more heavily or take away his gun.
It is not an irrational response, given the current state of our politics.

It does no good to yearn for an America that no longer exists, especially since pluralism and geographical and social mobility have created
much that we love about the United States. But if our politics is to get better, it is crucial that we recognize that the fragmentation of American society has made our public life much more difficult. We need to find ways
to tie citizens back into public life, not to turn them off even more. Above
all, we need to end the phony polarization around the issues of the 1960s
that serves only to carry us ever further from a deliberative, democratic
public life.

# 8

# Political Contributions Determine Election Outcomes

## Thomas Ferguson

*Thomas Ferguson is a professor of political science at the University of Massachusetts, Boston, and the author of* Golden Rule: The Investment Theory of Party Competition and the Logic of Money-Driven Political Systems, *from which this viewpoint is excerpted.*

The Republican party won control of Congress in the 1994 election not because of their ideology but because they succeeded in attracting campaign donations from big business. Analysis of Federal Election Commission reports on campaign fund-raising shows that Republicans raised more money than Democrats during the crucial final weeks of the election campaign. The commission reports also show that the Republican party funneled money to its candidates locked in close races. The raising and allocation of campaign funds determined the outcome of the election.

> Our issues are basically safe now, the health mandates, the employer mandates, the minimum wage. . . . I don't think those will be high priorities in a Republican Congress.
>
> GOPAC Contributor Thomas Kershaw
>
> Described by the *Boston Globe* as "a $10,000-a-year charter member" of Newt Gingrich's "grand effort to engineer a Republican takeover of Congress."*

Down through the ages, survivors of truly epic catastrophes have often recounted how their first, chilling presentiment of impending doom arose from a dramatic reversal in some feature of ordinary life they had always taken for granted. Pliny the Younger's memorable account of the destruction of Pompeii and Herculaneum by an eruption of Mt. Vesuvius in A.D. 79, for example, remarks how, in the hours before the volcano's final explosion, the sea was suddenly "sucked away and apparently forced back

. . . so that quantities of sea creatures were left stranded on dry sand."[1]

Sudden, violent changes in an ocean of money around election time are less visually dramatic than shifts in the Bay of Naples. But long before the Federal Election Commission (FEC) unveiled its final report on the financing of the 1994 midterm elections, it was already clear that in the final weeks before the explosion that buried alive the Democratic Party, changes in financial flows occurred that were as remarkable as anything Pliny and his terrified cohorts witnessed two thousand years ago: A sea of money that had for years been flowing reliably to Congressional Democrats and the party that controlled the White House abruptly reversed direction and began gushing in torrents to Republican challengers.

## An unforeseen sea change

Throughout most of the 1993–94 "election cycle" a reversal of these proportions seemed about as likely as the sudden extinction of two important Roman towns did to Pliny's contemporaries. The Republican Party, virtually everyone agreed, normally enjoyed a lopsided overall national advantage in campaign fundraising. But in the Congress, incumbency was decisive. Because big business, the Democratic Party's putative opponent, ultimately preferred "access" over "ideology," Democratic Congressional barons could reliably take toll—enough to make them all but invulnerable for the indefinite future.[2]

In addition, the Democrats now also controlled the White House. By comparison with its recent past, the party was thus exquisitely positioned to raise funds for the 1994 campaign. It could extract vast sums of "soft money" (funds allegedly raised for state and local party-building purposes, but in fact closely coordinated with national campaigns) from clients (i.e., patrons) in the business community. It could also exploit the unrivalled advantages occupants of the Oval Office enjoy in hitting up big ticket individual contributors.

> *In the long run, "access" eventually leads to favorable policy outcomes—or the money goes elsewhere.*

The glib contrast between "access" and "ideology" was always at best a half-truth. Particularly if one reckons over several election cycles, the differences in total contributions flowing to a Democratic leader who literally opened for business, such as former House Ways and Means chair Dan Rostenkowski, and a populist maverick like outgoing House Banking Committee chair Henry Gonzalez, are quite fabulous. Between 1982 and 1992, for example, FEC figures indicate that Rostenkowski succeeded in raising more than four million dollars in campaign funds. Over the same period, Gonzalez's campaigns took in less than $700,000. Among Democratic Congressional leaders, Rostenkowski's was far from a record-setting pace. Not including funds formally raised for his forays into presidential politics, Richard Gephardt, formerly House majority leader and now minority leader, raised over seven million dollars in the same stretch.[3]

Differences of this order demonstrate that, in the long run, "access" eventually leads to favorable policy outcomes—or the money goes elsewhere. Airy talk about mere "access" also subtly diverted attention from the historically specific stages of the accommodation between the Democrats and big business as the New Deal System died its painful, lingering death of 1,000 contributions.[4]

## The shift in campaign contributions

Early reports by the FEC for the 1993–94 election cycle appeared to confirm the conventional wisdom. In August 1994, the FEC released a survey of national party fundraising efforts (a much narrower category than the name suggests, since it takes no account of, for example, the separately tabulated efforts of individual campaigns for Congress, where the consolidated totals run far higher). This indicated that the Republicans were continuing to cling to their overall lead. Fundraising by the national Democratic Party, however, was up by 34 percent compared to the same period in 1991–92, when George Bush was president.[5]

In the bellwether category of soft money, one of the best available indicators of sentiment among America's largest investors, the contrast in regard to the same period was even sharper: Democratic receipts had doubled, to $33 million, while GOP receipts were down 28 percent, to a mere $25 million.[6]

Early statistics on Congressional races indicated much the same trend. One FEC report released during the summer of 1994 showed the early flow of contributions to Democratic candidates in all types of races—incumbencies, challenges, and, especially, open seats—running well above the levels of 1991–92. By contrast, House Republican candidates in every category trailed well behind their Democratic counterparts in average (median) total receipts. Other FEC statistics indicated that in House races, corporate political action committees (PACs) were tilting strongly in favor of Democratic candidates.[7]

As late as October, reports continued to circulate in the media of persisting large Democratic advantages in fundraising in regard to both Congressional races and soft money.[8] By then, however, little puffs of smoke were appearing over Mt. Vesuvius. Leaks in the press began to appear, suggesting that the Republicans, led by the redoubtable Newt Gingrich, were staging virtual revivals with enthusiastic corporate donors, lobbyists, and, especially, PACs.[9]

*Most election analysts in the United States habitually confuse the sound of money talking with the voice of the people.*

On November 2 came what could have become the first public premonition of the coming sea change: New figures for soft money published by the FEC indicated that between June 30 and October 19, the Democrats had managed to raise the almost laughable sum of 10 million dollars, while the Republicans had pulled down almost twice that much. Alas, the media and most analysts concentrated on each party's now closely similar take over the full two-year cycle. No one asked what had happened to dry up money to the Democrats in a period in which most observers still took for granted continued Democratic control of at least the House. Neither did anyone think to project the new trend, which was undoubtedly gathering additional fierce momentum in the final, delirious weeks of fundraising as the GOP scented victory.[10]

Two days later, the Commission published data on Congressional races throughout October 19. Though almost no one noticed, the new data pointed to a startling turnabout: Funds to House Republican challengers and candidates for open seats were now pouring in at approximately twice the rate of 1992. Democratic totals were up only slightly, save for a somewhat larger rise among candidates in races for open seats (that, unlike 1992, left their median receipts well behind those of their GOP counterparts).[11] The ceaseless drumbeating by Newt Gingrich and other Republicans was beginning to pay off. Only a few months before, corporate PACs investing in House races had been sending 60 percent of their funds to Democrats. By October, the PACs, along with other donors, were swinging back toward the GOP.

## Fundraising makes the difference in close races

The trend was strongest where it probably mattered most: in races waged by challengers and candidates for open seats. A study by Richard Keil of the Associated Press indicates that in 1992 PACs as a group favored Democratic challengers and open-seat aspirants by a 2 to 1 margin. By October 1994, however, the AP found that PACs had switched dramatically: More than half of their donations to challengers and open-seat aspirants were going to GOP candidates. The Associated Press figures are for PACs as a group, and thus include contributions from Labor PACs, which give lopsidedly to Democrats. The real size of the shift within the business community and related ideological PACs is, accordingly, significantly understated.[12]

Pressed by Gingrich, who wrote what the AP described as a "forceful memo" on the subject to would-be Republican leaders of the new House, the GOP also made efficient use of another emergency fundraising vehicle: the shifting of excess campaign funds from Republican incumbents with a high probability of reelection. Additional last minute spending against Democratic candidates also appears to have come from organizations "independent" of the parties, but favoring issues firmly associated with Gingrich and the Republicans, such as the recently founded Americans for Limited Terms.[13]

With so many races hanging in the balance (the Republicans, in the end, garnered only 50.5 percent of the total vote, according to a study by Stanley Greenberg for the Democratic Leadership Council [DLC]), the tidal wave of late-arriving money surely mattered a great deal. But the AP's striking analysis of the effects of this blitz underscores just how wide of the mark were the establishment pundits who rushed to claim that "money can't buy everything" in the wake of razor-thin defeats suffered by high-visibility, high-spending Republican Senate candidates in California and Virginia.[14]

The AP examined sixteen House contests decided by four percentage points or less. Campaign funds from Republican incumbents to other Republican candidates came in at three times the rate of donations from Democratic incumbents to their brethren. The Republicans won all sixteen. Even more impressive, of the 146 Republicans estimated by the AP to have received $100,000 or more in PAC donations, 96 percent were victorious—a truly stunning result when one reflects that much of the late money was clearly funnelled into close races.[15]

Most election analysts in the United States habitually confuse the sound of money talking with the voice of the people. Thus it was only to be expected that as they surveyed the rubble on the morning after the election, many commentators gleefully broadjumped to the conclusion that the electorate had not merely voted to put the Democratic Party in Chapter 11 [bankruptcy], but had also embraced Newt Gingrich's curious "Contract with America." But the evidence is very strong that it's still "the economy, stupid," and that the 1994 election was essentially the kind of massive no-confidence vote that would have brought down the government in a European-style parliamentary system.

## Notes

\*    The Kershaw quotation, which along with the paper's description forms the epigraph, appeared in the *Boston Globe*, November 20, 1994. The article noted that Kershaw's holdings include the Bull and Finch Pub of Boston, which inspired the "setting of the 'Cheers' television show." GOPAC is a vehicle for various organizing efforts of Gingrich's.

Some advice proffered by Gingrich on a GOPAC "training tape" for other would-be GOP candidates is of considerable interest from the standpoint of the discussion in the appendix of Thomas Ferguson's *Golden Rule: The Investment Theory of Party Competition and the Logic of Money-Driven Political Systems* on "rational expectations" and conditions of public debate in the United States. "'A shield issue is just, you know, your opponent is going to attack you as lacking compassion,' Gingrich says on the tape [provided to the newspaper]. 'You better find a good compassion issue where, you know, you show up in the local paper holding a baby in the neonatal center, and all you're trying to do is shield yourself from the inevitable attack.'"

This strategy absolutely requires the cooperation of the press to be effective.

1.    Pliny's description appears in his letter to Cornelius Tacitus, in *Pliny: Letters and Panegyricus*, trans. Betty Radice (Loeb Classical Library; Cambridge: Harvard University Press, 1969), vol. 1, p. 443.

2.    Because the introduction to Ferguson, *Golden Rule,* references so many discussions of campaign finance, there is no point in detailed citations to the campaign; but on the expected primacy of incumbents, see, e.g., the *Washington Post*, November 3, 1994. Note also that, of course, the advantages entrenched incumbents enjoyed were considered to be stronger in the House; many recognized that the Senate could easily go Republican.

3.    The campaign finance totals come from the Federal Election Commission; they are arrived at by summing the appropriate figures for total receipts in the Commission's various final reports on financial activity for the years indicated. Note that fees received from speaking, stamp sales,

and other activities are not included in these figures. These would almost certainly considerably increase the disparities.

4. See the discussion in chapters 5 and 6 of Ferguson, *Golden Rule*.

5. See the statistics presented in the FEC press release of August 8, 1994.

6. Ibid.

7. For the Congressional races, see the FEC press release of August 12, 1994, especially the comparative figures on median receipts for House candidates on p. 4; for the party balance among (House) corporate PAC contributions, see the FEC release of September 19, 1994 (the data reflect contributions through June 30; the exact percentage varies slightly depending on whether one calculates figures for only 1994 or through the whole cycle to that point), especially p. 4. Note that donations to GOP Senate candidates, where many observers saw a chance of a GOP turnaround, unsurprisingly held up very well.

8. In a spirit of collegial goodwill, let us dispense with specific references. See, instead, the surprise various commentators registered after the election in, e.g., Richard Keil's story of November 17, 1994, for the Associated Press. My reference is to the full text supplied to me by the AP; AP stories are often edited severely before running in local papers.

9. E.g., *Washington Post*, October 14, 1994.

10. See the FEC press release of November 2, 1994, which focused on the two-year totals. The real news comes only when one goes back and compares its statistics to those in the earlier FEC press release of August 8, 1994. It then becomes fairly clear that the real "break" in the trend of soft money probably came in the late spring or early summer. This is well before any widespread anticipation of the GOP takeover of the House, and is thus of considerable interest. What happened?

   In the absence of the FEC's final report on the 1994 election, it is difficult to be sure. Because the available evidence defies brief summary, all that is possible here is to record my belief that two developments that were closely related to the great bond crash that roiled world markets in the spring of 1994 played important roles in this shift of funds. First, the administration's policy of talking down the dollar against the yen drove a wedge between it and many of its supporters on Wall Street. Second, Congressional inquiries into hedge funds led other Wall Street supporters of the president either to switch to the GOP, or simply withdraw from previously made commitments to help finance the Democrats.

11. See the FEC press release of November 4, 1994, especially pp. 3 and 8. This constitutes, in my opinion, the truly clinching evidence for the late turn in funding House races, since it can be compared cautiously, but directly, with the earlier FEC release of August 12, 1994. Note that over the campaign as a whole, Democratic incumbents succeeded in raising very substantial sums.

12. See the AP story of November 15, 1994, by Richard Keil. I rely here on the full text the AP supplied me. I took considerable pains to resolve various

ambiguities in statistics the story reported. I am grateful to Keil for the patience and good humor he displayed in dealing with my queries.

13. On the excess campaign funds, see Keil's story for the AP of November 17, 1994, which also alludes to the Gingrich memo. Again, I rely on the uncut text supplied me by the AP. On the independent organizations, see, e.g., *Wall Street Journal*, November 4, 1994.

14. See page 1 of the draft dated November 17, 1994, of Greenberg's "The Revolt Against Politics," which accompanies his survey for the DLC discussed here.

15. See (the uncut text to) Richard Keil's stories for the AP of November 9, 15, and 17, 1994.

# Organizations to Contact

The editors have compiled the following list of organizations concerned with the issues debated in this book. The descriptions are derived from materials provided by the organizations. All have publications or information available for interested readers. The list was compiled on the date of publication of the present volume; names, addresses, and phone numbers may change. Be aware that many organizations take several weeks or longer to respond to inquiries, so allow as much time as possible.

**American Enterprise Institute for Public Policy Research (AEI)**
1150 17th St. NW
Washington, DC 20036
(202) 862-5914
fax: (202) 862-7178

This private research group studies and supports open and competitive markets, principles of limited government, and conservative cultural and political values. AEI publishes the bimonthly *American Enterprise* magazine, which contains statistics on public opinion and, occasionally, voting behavior.

**The Brookings Institution**
1775 Massachusetts Ave. NW
Washington, DC 20036-2188
(202) 797-6000
fax: (202) 797-6258

Founded in 1927, this liberal think tank conducts research and provides education in government, foreign policy, economics, and the social sciences. It publishes the *Brookings Review* quarterly, as well as numerous books and research papers.

**Center for a New Democracy (CND)**
410 Seventh St. SE
Washington, DC 20003
(202) 543-0773

CND is a nonprofit organization that seeks to increase political participation among Americans, to encourage a more responsive government, and to ensure that the electoral process is fair. It promotes campaign finance reforms that include limiting personal contributions to campaigns and increasing public funding of elections. The center publishes a monthly newsletter, *CND Update*, as well as fact sheets and policy papers on campaign finance.

**Center for Responsive Politics**
1320 19th St. NW, Suite 700
Washington, DC 20036
(202) 857-0044

This nonpartisan research group studies the role that money plays in federal elections and researches campaign finance reform issues, such as public funding of election campaigns. It publishes numerous books and booklets, including *Ten Myths About Money in Politics*, *A Brief History of Money in Politics*, and *Speaking Freely*.

### Committee for the Study of the American Electorate
421 New Jersey Ave. SE
Washington, DC 20003
(202) 546-3221

This nonpartisan group studies the decline of citizen participation in the political process and the decline in voting among the American electorate. It opposes reforms that propose to limit campaign fund-raising and spending because it believes this will limit voter involvement and political competition. It compiles and reports statistics on voting behavior.

### Funders Committee for Citizenship Participation
c/o Geri Mannion
Carnegie Corporation of New York
437 Madison Ave., 27th Fl.
New York, NY 10022
(212) 371-3200

The committee is an ad hoc group of individuals from various private foundations who seek to channel funding to programs that enhance voter education and participation. It publishes the semiannual newsletter *Funding Citizen Participation*.

### Kettering Foundation
200 Commons Rd.
Dayton, OH 45459-2799
(513) 434-7300
fax: (513) 439-9804

The foundation is a nonprofit research institution that studies problems of community, governing, politics, and education, with a particular focus on deliberative democracy. It publishes the quarterlies *Kettering Review* and *Connections* newsletter as well as the National Issues Forum book series.

### League of Women Voters
1730 M St. NW, Suite 1000
Washington, DC 20036-4505
(202) 429-1965
fax: (202) 429-0854

This voluntary organization promotes active citizen-participation in government and public policy making. Though it does not endorse candidates or political parties, it distributes information on candidates and issues and organizes voter registration and get-out-the-vote drives. The league publishes numerous booklets and pamphlets, including *Wired for Democracy: Using Emerging Technology to Educate Voters*, *Focus on the Voter: Lessons from the 1992 Election*, and *Getting the Most Out of Debates*.

**National Voting Rights Institute (NVRI)**
401 Commonwealth Ave., 3rd Fl.
Boston, MA 02215
(617) 867-0740

NVRI is a nonprofit organization that is challenging, through civil lawsuits, the constitutionality of the private financing of public elections. The organization believes that the influence of private money in elections prevents many poorer people from fully participating in the political process. It publishes the pamphlet *Challenging the Wealth Primary: Continuing the Struggle for the Right to Vote.*

**Third Wave**
185 Franklin St., 3rd Fl.
New York, NY 10013
(212) 925-3400
fax: (212) 925-3427
e-mail: 3Wave@nyo.com

Third Wave is a national organization of activists working to get young people more socially and politically involved in their communities. Its activities include voter registration drives among young people in low-income communities. It publishes a quarterly newsletter *See It? Tell It. Change It!*

**Twentieth Century Fund**
41 E. 70th St.
New York, NY 10021
(212) 535-4441
fax: (212) 535-7534

This research foundation sponsors analyses of economic policy, foreign affairs, and domestic political issues. It publishes numerous books and the report *1-800-PRESIDENT: The Report of the Twentieth Century Fund Task Force on Television and the Campaign of 1992.*

# Bibliography

## Books

| | |
|---|---|
| Alan I. Abramowitz and Jeffrey A. Segal | *Senate Elections*. Ann Arbor: University of Michigan Press, 1992. |
| W. Lance Bennett | *The Governing Crisis: Media, Money, and Marketing in American Elections*. New York: St. Martin's Press, 1992. |
| Walter Dean Burnham, ed. | *The* American Prospect *Reader in American Politics*. Chatham, NJ: Chatham House, 1995. |
| Stephen C. Craig | *The Malevolent Leaders: Popular Discontent in America*. Boulder, CO: Westview Press, 1993. |
| Alan Ehrenhalt | *The United States of Ambition: Politicians, Power, and the Pursuit of Office*. New York: Times Books, 1991. |
| Morris P. Fiorina | *Divided Government*. New York: Macmillan, 1992. |
| Jack W. Germond and Jules Witcover | *Mad as Hell: Revolt at the Ballot Box, 1992*. New York: Warner Books, 1993. |
| Newt Gingrich | *To Renew America*. New York: HarperCollins, 1995. |
| William Greider | *Who Will Tell the People: The Betrayal of American Democracy*. New York: Simon and Schuster, 1992. |
| Roderick P. Hart | *Seducing America: How Television Charms the Modern Voter*. New York: Oxford University Press, 1994. |
| Haynes Bonner Johnson | *Divided We Fall: Gambling with History in the Nineties*. New York: Norton, 1994. |
| Victor Kamber | *Giving Up on Democracy: Why Term Limits Are Bad for America*. Washington, DC: Regnery, 1995. |
| Michael Kazin | *The Populist Persuasion: An American History*. New York: BasicBooks, 1995. |
| Bruce E. Keith et al. | *The Myth of the Independent Voter*. Berkeley and Los Angeles: University of California Press, 1992. |
| Seymour Martin Lipset, ed. | *The Encyclopedia of Democracy*. Washington, DC: Congressional Quarterly, 1995. |
| David R. Mayhew | *Divided We Govern: Party Control, Lawmaking, and Investigations, 1946–1990*. New Haven, CT: Yale University Press, 1991. |
| Karen O'Connor and Larry J. Sabato | *American Government: Roots and Reform*. 2nd ed. Boston: Allyn and Bacon, 1996. |
| Kevin P. Phillips | *Arrogant Capital: Washington, Wall Street, and the Frustration of American Politics*. Boston: Little, Brown, 1994. |

| Nelson W. Polsby and Aaron Wildavsky | *Presidential Elections: Strategies and Structures of American Politics.* 9th ed. Chatham, NJ: Chatham House, 1996. |
|---|---|
| Samuel Popkin | *The Reasoning Voter: Communication and Persuasion in Presidential Campaigns.* 2nd ed. Chicago: University of Chicago Press, 1994. |
| Jonathan Rauch | *Demosclerosis: The Silent Killer of American Government.* New York: Times Books, 1994. |
| Mark J. Rozell and Clyde Wilcox, eds. | *God at the Grassroots: The Christian Right in the 1994 Elections.* Lanham, MD: Rowman & Littlefield, 1995. |
| Robert Schmuhl | *Demanding Democracy.* Notre Dame, IN: University of Notre Dame Press, 1994. |
| Gary W. Selnow | *High-Tech Campaigns: Computer Technology in Political Communication.* Westport, CT: Praeger, 1994. |
| Stephen Skowronek | *The Politics Presidents Make: Leadership from John Adams to George Bush.* Cambridge, MA: Harvard University Press, Belknap Press, 1993. |
| James A. Stimson | *Public Opinion in America: Moods, Cycles, and Swings.* Boulder, CO: Westview Press, 1991. |
| Ruy A. Teixeira | *The Disappearing American Voter.* Washington, DC: Brookings Institution, 1992. |
| Sidney Verba, Kay Lehman Schlozman, and Henry E. Brady | *Voice and Equality: Civic Voluntarism in American Politics.* Cambridge, MA: Harvard University Press, 1995. |
| Ben J. Wattenberg | *Values Matter Most: How Republicans or Democrats or a Third Party Can Win and Renew the American Way of Life.* New York: Free Press, 1995. |

## Periodicals

| Eric Alterman | "Clinton Rocked the Vote," *Rolling Stone*, February 23, 1995. |
|---|---|
| Paul Bedard | "Election '96! Third-Party Thunder," *The World & I*, November 1995. Available from 3600 New York Ave. NE, Washington, DC 20002. |
| Alan Brinkley | "Liberalism's Third Crisis," *American Prospect*, Spring 1995. Available from PO Box 383080, Cambridge, MA 02238-3080. |
| Peter Dreier | "Fear of Franchise: Detouring the Motor-Voter Law," *Nation*, October 31, 1994. |
| Geoff Earle | "The 'Motor Voter' Myth," *Governing*, August 1995. |
| David Frum | "The Elite Primary," *Atlantic Monthly*, November 1995. |
| Curtis Gans | "No Magic Bullets for Democratic Disaffection," *Social Policy*, Fall 1995. |

Marshall Ganz | "Voters in the Crosshairs: How Technology and the Market Are Destroying Politics," *American Prospect*, Winter 1994.

James L. Guth, John C. Green, Lyman A. Kellstedt, and Corwin E. Smidt | "God's Own Party: Evangelicals and Republicans in the '92 Election," *Christian Century*, February 17, 1993.

John Hood | "The Third Way," *Reason*, February 1993.

Joe Klein | "The New New Deal," *Newsweek*, December 26, 1994–January 2, 1995.

Jonathan Krasno and Donald Philip Green | "Stopping the Buck Here: The Case for Campaign Spending Limits," *Brookings Review*, Spring 1993.

Everett Carll Ladd | "The 1992 Election's Complex Message," *American Enterprise*, January/February 1993. Available from 1150 17th St. NW, Washington, DC 20036.

Everett Carll Ladd | "Of Political Parties Great and Small: A Dissent," *American Enterprise*, July/August 1994.

Lewis H. Lapham | "Thunder on the Right," *Harper's Magazine*, January 1995.

Michael Lind | "What Bill Wrought," *New Republic*, December 5, 1994.

Seymour Martin Lipset | "Malaise and Resiliency in America," *Journal of Democracy*, July 1995. Available from 1101 15th St. NW, Suite 200, Washington, DC 20005.

William G. Mayer | "America at the Polls: The Puzzle of 1994," *Current History*, March 1995.

Kevin Phillips, Celinda Lake, and Peter Overby | "One Nation Indecisive," *Common Cause Magazine*, Winter 1993.

Robert D. Putnam | "Bowling Alone: America's Declining Social Capital," *Journal of Democracy*, January 1995.

Jamin Raskin and John Bonifaz | "Equal Protection and the Wealth Primary," *Yale Law and Policy Review*, vol. 11, no. 2, 1993.

Arthur M. Schlesinger Jr. | "The Turn of the Cycle," *New Yorker*, November 16, 1992.

Ruy A. Teixeira | "Voter Turnout in America: Ten Myths," *Brookings Review*, Fall 1992.

Ruy A. Teixeira | "What If We Held an Election and Everybody Came?" *American Enterprise*, July/August 1992.

Jennifer Tomshack | "Leave the Dirty Laundry Out of the Voting Booth," *U.S. Catholic*, November 1995.

# Index

abortion, 12, 13, 50
African Americans, 14-15, 56
American Association of Retired People
  (AARP), 13
American society
  and alienation, 12
  fragmentation of, 63
  has lost faith in politicians, 35-36, 56
  is in decline, 10-12, 14-15, 38, 42
  is individualistic, 11, 36, 38, 59, 62
  puts political process before content,
    61
  values social concern and self-reliance,
    60
  see also citizenship
Associated Press (AP), 67, 69, 70

Bellah, Robert, 15
Bertrand, Claude-Jean, 23
*Boston Globe*, 64, 68
Burnham, Walter Dean, 53
Bush, George, 18, 41, 66
  defeat of, 45, 49
  1988 campaign of, 56
  supporters of, 50, 52

Canada, 35, 36, 37, 43, 44
Carter, Jimmy, 30, 50
Carter, Stephen, 54
Celeste, Richard, 29
Census Bureau, 28
Christian Right activists, 28
citizenship, 16, 20-25, 63
  has declined in U.S., 56
  is stronger in Canada, 37
  see also American society
Civil War, American, 57
Clinton, Bill, 18, 26, 51
  administration, 13
  as "new Democrat," 33
  and voters, 52
Cloward, Richard, 26, 27, 28, 32
*Confidence Gap, The* (Lipset & Schneider),
  35
conservatives. *See*
  Republicans/conservatives
"Contract with America," 68
Cuomo, Mario, 29

democracy, 24, 42-43, 61
  Americans losing faith in, 10-15, 56
  con, 16-25

conflict and consensus in, 53
needs "politics of remedies," 62
plebiscitary, 12, 13, 14
requires democratic culture, 11-12
*Democracy in America* (de Tocqueville),
  11
Democratic Leadership Council (DLC),
  67
Democratic National Committee, 28
Democratic Party, 19, 33, 39
  and bankruptcy, 68
  sources of support for, 42
  supported "Motor Voter" bill, 30
  supports contented majority, 41
  and voter registration, 26, 27, 28
  and voting rights movement, 33
  see also Democrats/liberals
Democrats/liberals, 40, 65
  and Catholic vote, 50, 51
  compared to British Labor Party, 43
  defend welfare state, 59
  and war, 42
Dionne, E.J., Jr., 55
Dukakis, Michael, 41
Dunne, Finley Peter, 22

Ehrenhalt, Alan, 24
elections, 12, 24, 46
  expense of, 41
  of 1994, 64-70
  outcomes of, determined by political
    contributions, 32, 64-68
  and representatives, 13, 19-20, 22-23
  see also voter participation
Elshtain, Jean Bethke, 10
Enthoven, Alain, 37
Environmental Protection Agency (EPA),
  23
Europe, 36, 43, 52, 57
  Eastern, 56, 61

Federal Election Commission (FEC), 64,
  65, 66, 68, 69
Ferguson, Thomas, 64, 68
Founding Fathers, America's, 19, 20

Galbraith, John Kenneth, 39
Gephardt, Richard, 65
Gingrich, Newt, 66
  and Americans for Limited Terms, 69
  and "Contract with America," 68
*Golden Rule* (Ferguson), 64, 68, 69

77